Telluride
The Sacred Valley

When you seek
the light
It
shall enlighten
your path.

Prabushri

Telluride
The Sacred Valley

Dr. Dennis L. Hunter

Credits:

Cover Design: Barbara A. Swanson, Pica² Graphics, Colorado Springs, Colorado
Photography: Dennis L. Hunter, Grand Junction, Colorado
Text Design and Composition: Barbara A. Swanson, Pica² Graphics
Editor and Project Manager: Sharon Green, Panache, Colorado Springs, Colorado
Printed by: Kendall Printing Company, Greeley, Colorado

ISBN: 0-9748650-0-1

Published by
Sacred Mountain Publishers
P.O. Box 3042
Grand Junction, Colorado 81502

For information regarding psychic readings mentioned in this book,
view the Website at
www.readingsfromthesource.com

Dedicated to

All those pilgrims who walk upon a sacred path
and the many teachers
who bring blessings and grace into our lives.

Contents

Prologue . . . . *ix*

Chapter 1   The Story Begins   1
Chapter 2   The Enchanted Hunt   15
Chapter 3   Cast Out of the Garden   29
Chapter 4   The Way of the World   49
Chapter 5   The Struggle for Dharma   61
Chapter 6   The Mountain Calls   71
Chapter 7   Home Again   81
Chapter 8   Invitations and Initiations   93
Chapter 9   The Conquest of Paradise   107
Chapter 10   Jaguar Kiva   117
Chapter 11   An Angel?   135
Chapter 12   The Hystory of a Quest   145
Chapter 13   Wodan's Fire   159
Chapter 14   Revelation Upon the Mountain   177
Chapter 15   Answered   195
Chapter 16   Winds of Change   209

Epilogue *216*
Glossary *221*

Prologue

I am here, absorbed within the unfolding blossom of morning meditation. There, beyond the window, lies the sacred mountain, engulfed in silence, relentlessly pulsing, barely visible through the gold, crimson, and violet mists of the beginning of another day. Late fall snows have sprinkled her with a dignity that seems to shimmer just beyond the capacity of human comprehension. Her power and beauty mesmerize a part of me that is just beginning to remember this promontory's origin and purpose. A few fading stars still twinkle through the hazy grey-blue, awaiting my response to the unfolding of the mountain's subtle wisdom.

Here in the valley, aspen and cottonwood trees stand motionless with naked, brittle branches stripped of life-giving leaves. Their rainbow gifts having been spent; they are cast into decaying, crucified earth. They quietly rest within the numbing darkness, waiting for the inevitable reward of spring's resurrection. I thrust open a window and draw in a chilling breath that startles lethargic lungs. Exhaling, I watch the cloud of my breath disappear into the rising morning fog of a river that the people once recognized as being sacred. I listen briefly to the rushing magic of what is now called the San Miguel River as it gurgles and rattles its way through the complex drama that has become known as the Telluride Valley. Soon the light of the sun will break over Ballard Peak. The radiant blessing will melt the fog and warm the earth, and the battle of the duality will continue.

Lost for a few moments in motionless contemplation, I suddenly become aware of an inquisitive blue jay. It looks at me with both accusation and expectation, reminding me of the mandate that has been given. I am amused at the bird's proud and almost arrogant posture. I am amazed at the vibrant intensity of the blue and black plumage. The scene seems all too perfect, too exacting, too precise, too alive to be reality. With one indignant hop, the blue jay once more rivets my wandering mind. He stares into my soul and I feel him wonder, "What is he waiting for?"

It seems presumptuous of me to actually begin compiling this chronicle. It seems preposterous that mere words may be capable of capturing the essence of the experiences, of the teachings, of the rememberings that have returned me to this sacred citadel.

Certainly there are many gifted and creative writers who could more easily tell the story. The thought of going through the relentless machinations of writing the book and finding a suitable publisher feels like an almost unnecessary distraction. Why would a person bother to take such a burden upon himself when right here, right now, the mountain and its many revelations draw me into its blissful communion.

Yet, the story springs forth and demands its expression. Slowly the resistance gives way. The story begins. It is writing itself. This shall be a manifestation of my "lana-lahti", a personal story of this soul's experience in the quest for spiritual reunification. It shall be what I would hope my grandchildren will remember of me after I am gone.

Chapter One

The Story Begins

Where does this story begin? Where does any story begin? The truth is, I can't recall a time when this story was not unfolding. It is a neverending story whose conclusion is only a prologue to an ever-expanding vision that is continually being called forth.

Ever since I can remember there has been a fascination with the legends of great spiritual quests. I have always felt drawn into the drama of the conquest for things of a spiritual nature. I recall being totally intrigued by the epic sagas of the judges, prophets, and prophecies of the King James Bible. As a child, movies like *The Ten Commandments*, *Ben Hur*, *The King of Kings* and many others would capture my imagination and fill me with wonder, for these historic accountings pose as many questions as answers.

Who were these sorcerers, holy men, and seers? Did God really speak to people through prophets and out of burning bushes? Is it possible to part an ocean with a prayer and the wave of a staff? Can pillars of fire be called down from the sky? Did angels really appear out of thin air and talk to people? Can people actually be raised from the dead?

Where had such magnificent people and miraculous events gone? Did these miracles really take place? Or were these stories merely insightful myths passed down through the generations, based on truth, but grossly exaggerated for the purpose of moral instruction?

In my life there did not seem to be any manifestation of such omnipotent spiritual power. It seemed to me that this spiritual heritage was based on something that had happened somewhere else, during a different age, to a different race, and within a different culture.

By the time I was in the fifth grade, Sunday school at Christ Church in Telluride had become a treasured habit. I still remember bolting frantically out the door, running across Main Street, and jogging through the alley to the little white church where I would be greeted by a beaming smile belonging to Mrs. Hancock. Except for Mom and Dad, you might say she was my first spiritual teacher. What I remember most about her is that she was a very gentle, loving lady. She really cared about the kids in her catechism class. She was incredibly patient and I never allowed myself to misbehave when in her presence. She had a consistent demeanor that didn't change or dissipate when church services were over. I still remember her warm and enthusiastic greetings, walking down the main street of our town or meeting us kids at the door of her home where we responded to invitations for an evening of singing and parlor games. The memory of her steaming, fresh-baked treats still lingers within my nostrils and upon my tongue.

One Sunday, there was a sermon about Elijah, the fiery prophet. God had sent him alone into the wilderness where he drank from a small brook that flowed into the Jordan River. Just as God had promised, ravens brought strips of fresh meat. Elijah's physical needs had not been forgotten. It was an example that when times are darkest, our God would always come through as long as we had faith and followed his commandments. Elijah and his contemporaries seemed to have a lot going for them. There seemed to be an abundance of angels and miracles. Wondering why I didn't see these things in my own experiences, I asked Mrs. Hancock about it. She confidently responded with familiar paraphrasing and suggested that if we simply asked in the name of Jesus, and truly believed, anything was possible.

Full of inspiration and Biblical images, I ran home, tore off my Sunday clothes and replaced them with a favorite plaid shirt and a comfortable pair of fading blue jeans. Balancing on a fallen log and precariously hopping across a few slippery rocks, I crossed the river into the pristine wilderness of the San Juan Mountains. I lunged up a narrow game trail near what has now become the base of the Coonskin ski lift.

There was a short, flat outcropping of large rock about a third of the way up the mountain. This was a favorite place where a long, narrow, glacial bench was alive with wild berries, thick grass, and towering trees. Dripping out of the outcropping was a small intermittent spring that trickled downward toward the San Miguel River. Before I had caught my breath, I slurped up a good portion of water from the puddle at the base of the rock. Wiping the icy droplets from my chin with my sleeve, I mounted the rock and launched into prayer after prayer, proclaiming my faith and commitment to the one God.

This is where I would make my stand. With the promise of Jesus I would find the miraculous God of Elijah. As I rambled on into the afternoon, the praying became much slower and more informal. Becoming weary and a bit hoarse, I concluded with the Lord's Prayer and sat expectantly waiting for my miracle. With considerable patience I calmly waited, looking for the ravens to appear, carrying my lunch.

Clouds were slowly forming over the mountains in preparation for the afternoon drizzle. I stretched back on the uncomfortable but indestructible rock of my faith and began to gaze upward into the stringy white puffs of clouds. Their quiet, lazy drifting was occasionally interrupted by the fierce rattling of green leaves that clung tightly to gently swaying aspen trees.

As a few drops of rain dripped from overhanging branches and onto my forehead, I realized I had fallen asleep. I sat up, looking around for the birds. They were obviously late, but I understood that I was being tested. Sitting on the rock of my faith, I looked into the heavens and continued to wait on my Lord, just like Elijah had done in the painted picture in my mother's Bible. The drips eventually became a chilling shower. Still undaunted, I hugged my knees into my chest and fought off growing feelings of doubt and awkwardness. I waited, waited again, and waited some more. I wondered if they had come and left while I had fallen asleep.

After a long while, the lyrical but demanding call of my mother drifted up from the valley floor. Looking down at West Pacific Street, I could see the toy-like house. It was wrapped in weathered tar paper that was made to look like brown bricks. On the back porch stood a rather irate sounding woman who was totally unaware of the sanctity of this hallowed occasion. I considered yelling down to her, explaining that I was sitting on this rock in the rain waiting for crows to bring me strips of fresh meat for lunch. Suddenly, the stark absurdity of the situation began to soften my brutal conviction. I don't think I would have liked eating strips of raw meat brought by ravens.

I didn't even have matches to build a fire for cooking. Still hesitant to admit defeat, I began searching for a plausible explanation. Perhaps God didn't respond to everyone in the same way. Recalling the phrase, "Many are called but few are chosen," I began to wonder if I was just one of the unlucky ones.

As my faith withered away, I began staring at my shoes and realized that these wet, muddy clogs were my Sunday-best. My panicked mind began searching for a reasonable explanation to my parents for such an oversight, but none was forthcoming. Being startled by my father's inflamed voice, "Where the hell is he?", I responded to the final incentive to shrink from the quest.

Acknowledging their search, I answered the parental call and slowly stumbled down the slippery ridge, feeling defeated and a bit humiliated. Whatever had happened, the blessing of God's miracles had eluded me. I later considered talking to Mrs. Hancock about it but felt stuck between not wanting to appear foolish and somehow not wanting to let her down.

*   *   *   *   *

Our pastor had become very ill with a Parkinson-like disease. The church elders were attempting to find a replacement, but apparently a new pastor couldn't be found. I imagine that our struggling little mining town had very little to offer in terms of money and housing. This feeble but stoic old man was trying to hang on until he could be relieved. Sometimes an attorney would journey from Ouray to present some ethical oratory. Sometimes a filmstrip would be shown. Somehow our minister kept his faith and poured his dwindling strength into his church, trying to keep it alive.

His voice would tremble and his hands would shake uncontrollably. The last time I recall him giving a sermon, he became so frustrated that tears began to well up in his eyes.

He had dropped his notes and no matter how hard he tried, his fumbling hands couldn't pick them up. He left the podium hoping to salvage a bit of dignity, quietly sobbing that he was sorry, but he couldn't continue. I watched him stumble down the aisle, clinging to the edges of the pews. The scene was pathetic. I wanted to look away, but a more dominant part of me just kept looking.

The five- or six-person choir had a couple of false starts as it began to choke out a familiar hymn. The two dozen or so adults in the congregation began to squirm uneasily and looked at the stained glass window or stared blankly at hymnals. It was as if no one could bear to be a witness to this failing, floundering warrior of God. I heard someone behind me frantically whisper, "My God, this is terrible. How can 'they' let this go on?"

Before he reached the back of the church, Mrs. Hancock bounced down the three or four steps from the choir loft, stretched open her arms, and embraced our black-robed pundit. Soon everyone was standing, hugging, and crying. I wondered how this loving, gentle man of God could become such a quivering, sobbing bag of bones. It seemed that his ravens hadn't shown up either. I could accept the fact that maybe I didn't have enough faith, but how could this thoroughly dedicated old man be so utterly abandoned? It reminded me of the crucifixion.

In fact, this dwindling little congregation had witnessed an exquisite crucifixion. Hearts had been touched deeply and there had been some emotional healing. It now occurs to me that it may have been the best sermon he ever gave. But I wondered if any of us would ever witness a resurrection as spectacular as this crucifixion. When Mrs. Hancock saw my trembling lips and the tears in my eyes, she surrounded me with the protective shroud of another hug. Reluctantly, I found myself yielding a bit and realized that her caring and sensitivity was much better than a few scraps from some old crow. Feeling the need for comfort and nurturing, I shuddered and relaxed a little and acknowledged my youthful immaturity.

However, the issue remained: Were the stories truth or were they fable? If this spiritual heritage was more than a Santa Claus for adults, there had to be much more to the story. I didn't know how, but I knew I had become even more resolved to rediscover it. After that particular Sunday, I didn't spend much time at the church, but I did spend a lot of time quietly reflecting on the stories of the Bible and exploring the mountains and streams that surrounded my home.

On some Sundays I would visit Oscar. Oscar was sort of an adopted granddad. His small weathered house was located on the south-facing slope above the Telluride Valley. He was fond of sitting on his sagging porch while slowly puffing on a well-seasoned pipe. Every so often the pipe would go out. Then from a watch pocket he would retrieve a blue-tipped wooden match. With three fingers and the edge of his thumbnail, he would gracefully ignite the sulphur tip. Placing the match to the bowl, the flickering orange flame would plunge deep into the moist tobacco. Soon a plume of white smoke would steam out of his nostrils and linger a moment under his narrow-brimmed hat. There was always the scent of burning sulphur and sweet-smelling tobacco around him.

He sat on a creaking, wooden chair that had been repaired with rusting wire, the same wire that had been used to temporarily lash the tie-rod together on his aging Willys Jeep. He would often push his hat back on his head, cross his legs, and gaze into Bear Creek Canyon and on up into the alpine basins. His gaze was so intent and serene that I sometimes wondered if he was seeing something that I had not yet found. Sometimes it was almost as if he had become absorbed within the mountain and it had become a part of his soul.

He kept a good supply of firewood right next to the door. There was a small axe wedged into the top of a stump where he would cut kindling before starting the fire in the kitchen stove. When chopping wood, he was fond of rolling up his shirt sleeves, which exposed the long sleeves of his flannel undershirt. When he was in the house he liked to put ashes from his pipe into the cuffs of his pant legs. He always offered me coffee. His wife, Lena, would usually scold him and hastily prepare some hot tea or cocoa. Sometimes Lena would put marshmallows on top of the hot chocolate. Oscar would laugh and exclaim that it looked fit for the King of Sweden.

In the afternoon he enjoyed sipping white wine. Swirling the precious liquid in an antique glass, he would spend as much time sniffing the aroma of the treasured brew as he did drinking it. Sometimes he would invite me to join him. This would usually bring even sterner admonishment from Lena. Oscar would lean forward with a hand on his knee, cock his head, and yell through the door, "Hell's bells, Lena, a little bit won't hurt him."

Sometimes I would take a little sip of the sour-tasting wine that stung my lips and burned my throat. I didn't really like it, but I didn't want to offend him. It was one of his ways of being friends. Watching me closely from the corner of his tilted hat, he would grin and tell me that I didn't have to drink it. Striking a philosophical pose, he would explain that a person was probably better off without it. He claimed that it was the nectar of the gods and he wasn't sure that mortals should be drinking it. However, that never seemed to stop him from enjoying it.

What astonished me the most is that he treated me like I was a grownup. He assumed that we were equals and never considered that he needed to convince me of anything. When I had something to say, it was always important to him. He would interrupt adults to make sure he understood my particular point of view. Sometimes he was more like a big brother than a surrogate grandfather.

He would tell me stories of the glory days when Telluride was a booming mining town. He described how his first wife had been killed near the Silver Bell saloon by a stray bullet during a disagreement between two miners. He once claimed to have hit a vein worth over $300,000, but he and his brothers spent it all and lost a ranch due to gambling. There was always the dream that someday he'd once again find that mother lode of a vein.

We both knew some of the stories were a bit exaggerated, but neither of us seemed to mind. However, years later, as gold approached $800 an ounce, some people supposedly took several hundred thousand dollars worth of "pay dirt" out of one of Oscar's claims that had been sold just a few years before. According to the story, they found the ore right where Oscar had said it would be. Oscar never had enough cash to drive the drift far enough to prove his theory.

I think most people saw him as a rather lethargic old-timer who never quite recovered from gold fever. However, my friend was obviously more enamored with the questing than the finding. I don't think finding gold had ever been a very important issue. It was just an excuse to live his lifestyle and roam the high mountain basins.

My dad and Oscar were partners in some mining claims located around Blue Lake in East Bridal Veil Basin. Roads were primitive at best, so two horses and a mule were bought for summer assessment work and prospecting. I don't think the animals were essential; Oscar just preferred them for the high country. They were good companions who could also carry provisions. Oscar had trained them to come to him by frequently offering them a good supply of oats from a tattered canvas feedbag. In the summer, the animals were often left to graze up around Bridal Veil and La Junta basins. This was near a claim where the horses could also be used by his two older brothers, Harry and Gator, who were also doing some prospecting.

One year, the snows came early. After two major storms, the horses were stranded. The narrow Jeep trail had become impassable. Ignoring the personal concerns and protests of well-meaning friends, Oscar drove to the base of Ajax and prepared to rescue the animals. He strapped on a homemade pack full of oats and carried snowshoes and old Nordic skis into the basin.

He said he found the black-maned mule in snow up to his belly. Billy, the pinto, was exhausted and it was difficult to get him back on his feet. The oats were a big help. Big Red was the strongest and broke the snow-packed trail for the others as they inched their way back down the mountain.

I'll never forget seeing Oscar leading the horses to the pasture in East Telluride. The animals were in poor condition and appeared to be a little snow-blind. Oscar had to have been in his late sixties or maybe older. He must have been exhausted. As he approached town, he grabbed the mane, swung a leg over Big Red, and rode him bareback right into a pasture where I later built my family home.

I've never seen any cowboy moviestar sit as tall as Oscar. I think Oscar sat a little taller because he knew I was watching. And he knew I understood. This wasn't just some old-timer with tall stories. This was a glimpse into another time when tough, proud men with magnificent dreams strode into the wilderness with all its beauty and treacherous challenge. This was a final epilogue, a time when you could look into the eyes of an old man and marvel at the wonders that he had seen. Since that day, this is the way I have always seen him, even after he aged and his health failed. The last time I saw him was in the summer of 1974 in front of the old Elks Club. He was sickly and emaciated, but his eyes still had that sparkle.

In the summer, Dad and I usually lived in a cabin south of Telluride near Priest Lake. This was where Dad was erecting his mill. There was no plumbing or electricity. We used to play chess by candlelight. One morning, I awoke with the sound of Dad's .38-caliber pistol exploding in my ears. A young buck had walked over to an intermittent stream of water near the portal of the San Juan Mine. My father had always preferred younger deer because the meat was more tender. As he eviscerated the animal, Dad began carefully checking the entrails for any sign of disease. Then he slowly began to tell me about an Indian friend he had known in Arizona.

They had been sharing some hunting stories while working in Dad's flagstone quarry just north of Williams, Arizona a few years before. This Navajo laborer had presented a Native American perspective on hunting. It isn't an uncommon idea, but it was new to me. I found it fascinating and learned something about my father that he had not previously shared with me. He explained that during a prayerful ritual it was the custom to speak to the spirit of the animal that was being sought. One should carefully think about the purpose of the hunt. It was important to reflect on whether or not the taking of life was necessary. He went on relaying the idea that sometimes an animal would sense the need and sincerity and allow itself to be sent to the hunter as a sacrifice to the hunter's purposes.

After slaying the animal, the hunter was supposed to give thanks and ask the animal's forgiveness while recalling the purpose of its sacrifice. It was important to be a gracious beneficiary and to use as much of the animal as possible. It would be an insult to discard anything that could be used. The spirit and power of the animal would nourish the body and merge with the spirit of the hunter. As hunter and hunted become one, there comes a sense of sacredness.

I could see that Dad found it a little awkward, as he fumbled with his words and tried to explain. He lacked confidence and wasn't sure his explanations made any sense. However, I easily understood and accepted what he was saying. He stood quietly over the slain deer for a moment and seemed to run out of words. Then he grinned broadly as we both realized that he was talking as much about himself as he was about the Indian.

It was not uncommon for Dad to rise before the sun. After shaking down the grates and getting the fire started in the kitchen stove, he liked to sit on the cabin step and smoke a cigarette. He had transplanted a small blue spruce next to the door. He seemed to be very content to just sit and look at it. Dad loved blue spruce. He used several of them for the rafters in the roof of his mill. He was fond of saying that they were straight as an arrow and grew straight up into the sky. As he sat on the step, flicking ashes from his cigarette, he sometimes thought out loud about what he hoped to accomplish during the day. I found it sort of amusing because on more than one occasion it appeared that he was talking to his tree.

This morning he had awakened thinking about what his Navajo friend had told him years before. When a buck appeared within a rock's throw of the cabin, he just couldn't resist the temptation. We had run out of camp meat and now there would be plenty. That morning a father and son had shared something that brought them a little closer.

It was summertime and this was not legal hunting season. I could tell that Dad felt a little uneasy about breaking the law. Although he didn't think too highly of government intrusions, he believed laws should be obeyed. However, he didn't see anything wrong with what he had done. From his point of view, he needed the meat and it had offered itself to him. As it turned out, Dad got caught. A court date was set.

A few days after the incident, I was back in Telluride playing with some neighborhood friends. I had been told over and over again not to go into the woodshed behind the house. We had always played in that shed whenever we wanted, so it seemed like a rather strange request. As we started playing "kick the can" the curiosity became overwhelming, so I took a peek and got caught.

The panicked look on my friend's face said it all, but I didn't fully appreciate the situation until I got home. A six-point buck had been hanging in the shed with the hide still on it. And it still wasn't anywhere near hunting season. I mentioned the incident during dinner. I remember being rather impressed with the size of the antlers. Dad got a rather amused look on his face. The buck was in the shed of the home of the person who would be judging Dad's poaching charges.

I remember the magistrate looking nervous and saying, "You know, Dan, I have no choice; I have to do this." Dad grinned and said he understood. He pled no contest and paid the required fine. They were later seen laughing and drinking at the Elks Club. To the best of my knowledge, that was the only time Dad did any poaching.

Chapter Two

The Enchanted Hunt

When it came to hunting, Dad was a marvel. The power of his concentration seemed to enshroud the entire landscape. It was as if his entire manhood hung upon his ability to bring home his quarry; it was as if he had lost himself and could not rest until sacrificed blood would release him from his obsession. Afterward, a sort of contentment would descend upon him. He would express his appreciation to be able to participate in the reaffirmation of the inevitable cycles of life. However, he would never use those kinds of words. He would just make some short intermittent comments while taking a break from butchering, or perhaps he would wax a bit philosophical while gazing into a simmering pot of freshly prepared stew that he was slowly stirring.

One year he took me hunting near Norwood, Colorado, just north of the San Miguel River. We hadn't seen anything all morning. It was after noon when he slowed the Jeep and began to scan the side of a hill in the distance. He told me there were twelve to fourteen deer grazing just below the saddle of the gently sloping ridge that sprawled out to the edge of a sizable canyon. I looked and looked but couldn't see a thing. If there really was a herd where he was pointing, it was much too far for our rifles to reach.

Finally, in exasperation, he dug out a battered pair of binoculars and asked me to take a look. Soon I spotted two or three, but didn't see the bucks that he claimed were there. Steadying the binoculars on the open door of the Jeep, he scanned the ridge for what seemed like an hour. Shaking off his rigid concentration, he looked at me for a moment, then nudged me in the ribs with an elbow. With a slight chuckle he said he had a good idea of where the deer were going.

We drove a mile or two down the rutted logging trail and stopped near a cluster of tall scrub oak. The twisted grey trunks still had a few brown and orange leaves clinging to their branches. Dad swung his legs out of the Jeep, made a small fire, and proceeded to cook a late lunch. He always preferred hot food. Leaving me to clean up, he laid down on his bedroll, which he had placed next to a decaying old tree that looked like it had been struck by lightning. He pulled a large pocket knife from his back pocket, opened it up and gently inspected the razor-sharp edge with the tip of his thumb. Then he sternly told me that I shouldn't ever do that because I might cut myself. Picking up a small branch that had fallen from the lifeless tree, he carved a toothpick that remained in the corner of his mouth the rest of the afternoon.

Dad told me that there were two ways of hunting. He was fond of saying, "A person can wander around all over the whole country and never see a damn thing." To him it was more important to pay attention to what was right in front of us rather than to wear ourselves out stampeding through endless miles of wilderness. Otherwise, he explained, by the end of the day you come home cold, tired, and empty handed.

Dad said that his way of hunting was to try to understand things from the deer's standpoint and figure out where the deer would want to go. Then you simply put yourself on their path and wait for them to come to you. He claimed that this more relaxed approach allowed the opportunity for the mountain to decide which deer it wanted you to have.

After pausing for a long satisfying yawn, Dad laid back on his bedroll and propped a stained pillow up against the tree. A moment later he took his boots off, placed his John Wayne-style hat over his face, and drifted off into his afternoon nap. I remained a bit skeptical about his method of hunting because I knew Dad had a strong tendency toward lethargy.

For the longest time I sat motionless on matted grass listening to the rhythmic rattles and whistles of my father's snoring.

As he groaned and rolled over, I gradually became aware of the ebb and flow of the wind through the trees and underbrush. Gazing at the tree where Dad was sleeping, I wondered what it would have been like to have been here when the lightning struck. I wondered how long the fire had burned within its trunk and branches. I wondered if a summer rain had helped put the fire out.

I listened to chattering birds that were flittering through the branches of an evergreen. They were squabbling over some squirming morsel that was probably plucked from the forest floor. A harried squirrel scampered over brittle leaves and disappeared behind a fractured boulder. I became aware of my breathing and began to hear my heart beating.

All the time that this was going on, there was a continuous throb of motionless silence that served as a relentless backdrop for this myriad of activity. I began to think of what Dad had told me about his method of hunting. I thought of all the things that we missed when we were noisily bouncing along in the Jeep. This may have been my first lesson in meditation. Soon, I too fell into a deep sleep.

I awoke to an abrupt tapping on the side of my boot. Dad handed me a rifle, the .30-.30 Winchester. He grinned and said in a voice hoarse and raspy from smoking too many cigarettes, "Come on, ol' buddy, I think it's time to take a walk." I could tell by the way he motioned me toward the rutted logging trail that it was time to move quietly. It had become cloudy and a winter chill was hanging in the air. Watching the clouds, I wondered if it might snow. I stepped on a loudly cracking branch. Dad's head jerked around. He glared at me with a face that was full of accusation. The intense volatility in his eyes commanded my entire attention and obedience.

All was serious now. He had become transformed into the hunter. I carefully followed behind, choosing my steps more carefully. He left the logging trail and began to follow a gently sloping ridge. After four or five hundred yards he waved me forward and indicated that he wanted me to stay to his left. You could hear a gust of crisp wind coming our way as it began to swell through the trees. I zippered up my coat and buttoned the collar tightly around my neck. Suddenly, a small rock bounced off my right shoulder. I turned and there was Dad squatting next to a withered clump of sage. He was peering under the lower branches of the forest. Pointing cautiously, he directed my attention down the path. Up ahead I could see a small watering pond constructed for cattle.

Then I saw them. There must have been at least a dozen. Less than fifty yards away stood a four-point buck. I still remember Dad's large beaming grin. He knew my skepticism regarding his hunting methods. His honor had been clearly vindicated. Assuming a kneeling position, I clumsily slammed my knee down on a rock, but I was too full of adrenaline to care about the pain. I jammed the butt of the rifle into my shoulder and took a deep breath, then slowly let it out. The antlered head jerked up. It ran a few steps and then stopped. I looked back at Dad. He roared in a loud convulsive whisper, "He's all yours. Shoot! Shoot!"

The stag didn't run. He turned sideways and flashed his white tail to give warning to the others. As the rest of the deer bounced away, he stood there just staring at me. His dark eyes riveted my intensely focused mind. Forgetting that I had been slowly squeezing the trigger, I was startled when the rifle abruptly thundered with deafening ferocity and thumped against my clenched shoulder.

The deer briefly shuddered and collapsed with legs and head twitching. Running up to my target, I heard his last gurgling breath. Still mesmerized by the large dark eyes, I watched his pooling blood spread across the ground. This was my first deer. I was thirteen.

I felt helpless and no longer innocent. There was both a sense of excitement and revulsion. It was as if a savage, blatant truth had been revealed. For me to live, something has to die. Such truth could be embraced or ignored, but the truth remained and was unalterable. Perhaps this is the original sin. Perhaps the true original sin is not acknowledging the reality of our predatory nature and not giving something back in order to re-establish the balance.

As I watched the thick coagulating blood soak into the earth, I began to think of the crucifixion of the one we call Jesus. I began to think of the pastor. I wondered what it would be like when my time came to die. And always there were the large gentle eyes. They watched innocently, without judgment. Frozen in time, they recorded a moment of irrevocable decision. They surrendered to me with a trust that left a sense of haunting responsibility. They drew me into an odd kind of resignation and serenity that is always fading but never quite disappears.

Dad sensed the solemnity of my experience. He placed his hand on my shoulder, gave me a squeeze, and said, "Do you feel a little sad?" My head nodded as I acknowledged the awkward thickness in my throat. He told me to never forget that feeling. He said, "That feeling is the difference between a hunter and a sportsman." Slowly I regained my composure. Dad presented the large folding knife that he kept in his back pocket. With a slight tremble, I carefully opened the belly and watched the steaming warmth escape upward into the frigid air.

With candid instruction and welcome assistance, I proceeded to gut the carcass and prepare it for the trip home. Dad said that some people think you should eat the raw heart of the deer. It was supposed to give you strength and wisdom. He said he didn't see the need for that. Then he removed the liver and carefully wrapped it in a large handkerchief and said it would taste great with fried onions. He rubbed some of the blood on my cheeks and forehead. Then he winked and smiled. I realized my shoulders were clenched high around my neck; I took a deep breath and relaxed.

I began to feel a subtle but definite sense of pride and accomplishment, yet I was relieved that the ordeal was over. When I unloaded my weapon I carefully examined the cartridges; they looked very different than when I had placed them in the magazine. There emerged a sense of awe and respect. A sense of power and remorse.

Over the next few days the marvelous animal was transformed into carefully wrapped white packages of meat that disappeared into our freezer. The wildness and freedom of the animal was gone. But sometimes while eating dinner I would still feel the eyes and wonder if somewhere in the forest his spirit continued to live. I did know that somewhere in my heart he would live forever.

This was the way things were. It was a time when fathers and sons would go on pilgrimage into the wilderness in quest of something that was never given words. We would come home with something a little more meaningful than a dead carcass and a freezer full of meat. There was a sense of an ancient reenactment of pagan ritual. The taking of one's first deer was a rite of passage; and, if you could see deeply enough, there might be a recognition of the interconnectedness of all things.

As the seasons passed, I realized that the sportsmen had begun to come into our sacred hunting ground. These sportsmen are more like men trying to escape from something than men trying to find something. Their clothing is new and shiny and smells synthetic. Their creaking boots are inflexible and uncomfortable. They are often loud, arrogant, and vulgar. They bring their ignorance and poisons with them. They drag along an overabundance of equipment, gadgets, and gizmos that leave them always fumbling and arranging things. They appear unable to allow themselves the time to rapture in the joyous simplicity of sacred land. They too often remain clumsy and insensitive to the wilderness. There seems to be a sense of savage conquest and domination, a desire to conquer and pillage. These are the ones who come to clutch trophies. These are the ones who kill for the fun of it and leave carcasses rotting in streams. These are the ones who arrogantly cut off antlered heads and place them on urban walls where the nourishing spirit of the animal is never known. Sometimes I think that the sportsmen have continued to flourish and that hunters have become an endangered species.

Late one fall Dad and I and Oscar had gone over to the Ophir Valley to get firewood for the winter. Almost everybody still used wood and coal for both heating and cooking. A year or two before there had been tremendous snowslides. Several collapsing houses in the town of Ophir had been catapulted off their foundations. Avalanches that hadn't been active for decades had begun to run. Back then I don't think I knew what avalanches were. We had always called them snowslides. Huge piles of shattered trees had been strewn in several locations throughout the valley. We had driven over the winding dirt and gravel road from Telluride in one of Dad's aging military trucks. He had planned to use them in his mining activities in the high country. They were great old trucks with six-wheel drive. I remember helping load a seemingly endless stream of foot-long pieces of timber. As my head throbbed from the high-pitched whine of Dad's new McCullough chain saw, I realized we could easily do several loads of cut firewood in one day.

It was hunting season and Oscar had made the trip to Ophir in his faded green Jeep. Inside the homemade aluminum cab he fondled a new rifle that he hoped would bring him success. He had finally given in to the idea of hunting with an optical sight. Admitting that his eyes weren't as good as they used to be, he carefully cleaned the dust from the lenses of the scope. He announced that he had decided to return to Telluride by way of the Alta Lakes, which was a road that wound up close to timberline and then meandered through what is now Telluride Mountain Village Resort. Then the trail plunged down Boomerang Hill into the Telluride Valley.

Early evening was approaching. Oscar began complaining that he couldn't seem to find anyone who wanted to go hunting. Dad winked at me and asked if I knew anyone who would like to go along. As they began to chuckle, I grabbed my jacket and jumped into the passenger side of Oscar's Jeep.

Coming out of the Ophir Valley, we turned north and were soon zigzagging our way up the Alta road. Our eyes strained for a glimpse of any game that might be encountered along the trail.

Judging from the tire tracks, several vehicles had been patrolling the area hoping to fill their license. It was cold and the road was rutted and becoming dusty. It was not unusual for Oscar to remove the doors to his aluminum cab during hunting season. The deep treaded tires of the Jeep threw up a small cloud of dust that slowly dissipated behind us. My hands were clenched tightly in my pockets. My nose and ears had grown red and numb. The thin mountain air was dry and made my face feel tight. The lining of my nose was irritated. You could feel the grit between your teeth.

My feet were braced against the floor helping to keep my balance while sitting on an old pillow that covered broken springs. Something squeaked and rattled every time we hit a bump. As we bounced along in the noisy Jeep we remained silent. The snows were late, but dark and massive clouds were descending from the peaks. As we approached the Alta basin, the clouds began to billow southward toward Ophir and Ilium valleys.

Oscar drove past the old mining camp and stopped near the lakes to stretch his legs. He opened a thermos of coffee that was still warm enough to emit a brief puff of steam. Carefully rubbing the stubble on his face with the palm of his left hand, he began studying the weather. The other hand held the red plastic cup from the thermos. An unexpected gust of wind ripped his hat from his head. He splashed the coffee on the ground and threw the cup on his seat. Cursing, he chased the hat a few yards before retrieving it. He came back to the Jeep and offered me the use of a heavier coat that was stashed under an old tarp behind his seat. I gratefully put it on. I think he had planned to use it himself. We took a short walk, sometimes kicking at rocks, occasionally picking up low-grade pieces of ore to examine for minerals.

I think I was more interested in visiting the Alta mining property than going hunting. At that time the ghost town of a mining camp was nearly intact. There were numerous cabins and an old boardinghouse that had been used for the Gold King and Black Hawk mines. There was even a one-room schoolhouse. In addition to the buildings that were used for mining operations, there were three or four well-constructed homes where the engineers and supervisors had lived. They were still occupied in the summer months by people that were remilling the old dumps.

The large beaver ponds produced a good crop of mosquitoes, but an even better crop of trout. The view from Alta toward Sunshine and Wilson peaks is truly magnificent, especially when the sun's golden rays outline the snow-crusted granite peaks during pink sunsets. But this day the sunset was hidden and billowing clouds continued to darken the horizon.

I knew what was on his mind. The road past the lakes was very primitive and rarely used. In places it was a mere path between trees. With the rapid change of weather and the distant setting of the sun, there was a chance of getting into serious trouble. It was wise to stop and consider the changing weather conditions. A shroud of quarter-sized snowflakes began to tumble down from the peaks. Visibility faded.

After a few moments Oscar erupted with his usual animation. "Hell's bells, Danny!" He called me by my father's name. He considered me to be little Danny, or Danny Junior. "A couple a old mount'n men like us 'otta' be able ta git through a few miles a blowin' snow. It'd take just as long to go back the other way, and we'd still have ta drive fifteen miles 'round the mount'n ta git home."

Actually it was only about ten miles. As we climbed back into the Jeep, the snow was already an inch or two deep. Oscar started the engine and eased forward. I was glad that he decided to go on. The blowing snow was rhythmically brushed away by the single windshield wiper located on the driver's side. I gazed out the open door, watching the swirling white torrent. The course had not been maintained for years. At times it was hard to see the path. Once we had to get out to move a fallen tree. Another time Oscar took a short detour around a section of road that was badly eroded.

Before too long we reached the crest of the ridge on the west shoulder of Bald Mountain. The full force of the squall was numbing our faces. Although I could see some concern on Oscar's face, he didn't seem particularly worried. It was as if he were invigorated and challenged. It was as if he had shifted into another plane of existence and was more aware, more alive. I began to understand that this was the kind of adventure that made his life challenging and worthwhile.

We came to an abrupt stop and I banged my head on the window. Oscar leaped out of the Jeep and looked at the undercarriage. We were off the path and had run over a decaying stump. He wandered back and forth through the frosted trees for a few minutes and found where we had left the snow-covered trail. Laughing at himself, he backed up and we continued our journey.

We were now descending into a heavily wooded area on the Telluride side of the mountain. Pine trees became interspersed with aspens. There was a series of relatively flat marshy areas that ranged from one to several acres. Water would collect from the melting snow into tiny intermittent streams that flourished within these secluded meadows. There was excellent grass and cover and numerous small beaver ponds, but nothing very large or deep. However, if we got too far off the trail, getting stuck would almost be a certainty. This is where Oscar had hoped to do some hunting.

The last glow of the sun was filtering through a fog of lightly falling snow. This created a strange pearl-gray light, which seemed to radiate from everywhere. The depth and rate of snowfall continued to decrease as we coasted down the mountain in the low range of four-wheel drive. My skin no longer felt dry and tight. The air had become fresh, moist, and invigorating. As I sat back in the seat, the muscles in my legs, back, and arms began to relax. Oscar must have felt the worst was over for he began to tell one of his marvelous stories.

As we rounded a turn, we pulled out of a thick grove of pine trees and approached the edge of another little meadow. As I began a deep and refreshing yawn, a huge bugling elk appeared less than a hundred feet from our vehicle. Oscar immediately killed the engine. Instinctively, he reached back behind the seat looking for the rifle that I was already uncovering. When I held the weapon out to him, he grabbed the gun and eagerly hugged it into his shoulder.

The animal was magnificent; it was almost terrifying. It lowered its head and glared at us with moist breath boiling out of its nostrils. I wondered if bull elk ever charged. The rack was tremendous. It was even bigger than any I'd seen hanging in the Elks Club. The beast shook his head defiantly. But all this was not the most startling characteristic. The animal was white. Pure white. It was as pure as the driven snow.

Oscar was mesmerized. He sat motionless. My heart was thundering. I tried to imagine what was going on in Oscar's mind. This was the opportunity of a lifetime. This would be a trophy that could adorn the halls of the Telluride Elks Club for a hundred years. This would be the story of stories. This would be a story of living proof. Oscar might even become a legend. I pulled my shoulders up around my ears and waited for the thunder of the rifle. My eardrums began to clench. Then they felt like they were twitching and fluttering in anticipation of the thunderbolt that would soon explode from the tiny aluminum cab. I swallowed and held my breath.

Then Oscar lowered the gun and just watched. After a moment, the white beast snorted and broke his wild-eyed stare. He pawed at the ground and proudly arched his neck and once again began gently shaking his great antlered head. He hesitated briefly, turned, and walked into a quiet flurry of swirling white snow. The animal faded and dissolved into the wilderness. I stared intently into the luminous fog. My incredulous mind wondered if what it had just witnessed was real.

Oscar suddenly remembered my presence, slowly turned, and inquired, "Did you see that?"

I replied, "I think so." I asked if he'd ever seen a white elk before. He didn't answer the question.

He just looked toward the valley for a few moments, then looked into my face and said, "Over the years I've seen a lot of things in these mountains. Some of them are hard to explain. Sometimes I don't even try." Then he slapped his leg and erupted with contagious laugher that echoed through the forest as he re-started the engine.

To this day I'm not sure if the event was real or an apparition.

We continued bouncing and sliding down the road. Oscar turned the headlights on a few hundred yards before we reached the Telluride Valley. Crossing the San Miguel River, we reached the highway and drove on into town.

Mom was relieved by our arrival. Dad had already returned home with the loaded truck along the usual route through South Fork. They had been nervously watching the storm. In town, there had been just a light sprinkling of snow. Lena had brought one of her special recipes over to the house for a potluck feast.

I waited for Oscar to tell the story. To my surprise, he just pushed back his hat and said, "Well, Danny spotted an elk, but I couldn't get a shot at it. I guess sometimes they just get away."

It was then that I knew Oscar was a first-class hunter. Changing the subject, he loosened his boot strings and started teasing Dad. He wanted to know why the firewood was still on the truck and hadn't been unloaded.

After dinner, Oscar lit his pipe and the four of them talked late into the night. I curled up on a rollaway bed that was wedged in the corner of the room near the wood-burning stove. I didn't understand it, but I knew that something very special had hap-pened. This was not some story about someone else in another time, in another place. This had happened to me. There had been some magic in my life. Miracles just might be possible. Contemplating the adventures of the day, I drifted off to sleep.

Chapter Three

Cast Out of the Garden

Every so often Dad's parents would visit from Iowa. Granddad had been a pioneer aviator. After the First World War he started a flying circus which began with one plane. The way he told the story, a check was written for two planes that were still in the crate. Before the check cleared, Granddad sold one of the planes for more than the cost of the two planes. He got his price because he also agreed to assemble the plane that he was re-selling. In this manner, Granddad was able to cover his check for the two planes and thereby purchase his own plane free and clear. During his life he opened several airports, was active during World War II, and taught thousands of people to fly. He wasn't what you would call wealthy, but he was adventurous, worked hard, and was financially comfortable. I always admired him for being able to make a successful business out of his favorite hobby.

Before we moved to Colorado, Dad visited the Telluride Valley in a single-engine Cessna. He liked to land on the road just outside of town. He and Oscar had a great time flying through the high alpine basins, supposedly trying to map promising veins of ore across the mountain ridges. There was some public criticism of using the public highway for landing. Dad claimed that he had engine trouble and needed to land to assess mechanical problems. After several episodes the authorities decided that Dad shouldn't fly that particular plane if it continued to have so much engine trouble.

One year these grandparents had been exploring the Southwest. We agreed to meet them in Gallup, New Mexico. It was a long dusty trip. The road from Telluride south to Cortez was gravel. There were sections that were narrow and rutted. It was definitely preferable not to travel too fast. Mom was fond of saying that the road was so rough it could shake your eyeteeth loose. We made the trip in a pink Jeep that Dad had bought the previous autumn. It was an outrageous color for that time. I think the only reason he bought it was to spite my mother. She had been pointing out the practical side a bit too often for Dad's comfort. After getting over the initial shock, it did seem to be a welcome change from the dozens of drab-green Jeeps that roamed the region.

*   *   *   *   *

After an early lunch in Cortez, we entered the high desert plateau. It was vast and expansive. The land seemed to extend forever. It was a dynamic contrast to the deep narrow valley that cradled Telluride. Time seemed to disappear as we crossed sandy red plains.

Occasional crimson mesas and towering rock spires broke up the monotonous landscape. It was a stark change from the mountains where water flowed everywhere and everything was green. For someone used to cooler temperatures, the heat was suffocating. The custom metal cab of the Jeep felt like a solar oven. We droned along at about forty-five miles an hour. Every so often Dad would swerve or zigzag back and forth across the road in order to avoid the larger potholes.

At times I wondered if Dad knew where he was going. I think Mom had some doubts too. A few times she began folding and refolding the road map. After long periods of examining the little red and black lines, she presented her estimate of where we were and pointed out our most probable location. Dad would just chuckle and say, "What's the matter; are you lost?" Dad had always prided himself on being an excellent land navigator, whether he knew where he was going or not.

The reservation highways were in deplorable condition. Some sections of the road were shattered and broken. Where it was an absolute necessity, there were a few narrow bridges. Culverts were rare and often full of silt. The wisdom of the time constructed the roadbed so that the "highway" would dip down and allow the infrequent flash floods to pass over the asphalt. There were several stretches where the sand had drifted over the road. The drifting sand reminded me of the snow we would drive through during the winter.

We stopped for gas at a trading post that probably vanished decades ago. Mom shoved open the door of the Jeep and removed a scarf that had been used to keep the grit off her hair. She wetted it under a dripping water faucet and rubbed it over her face and neck. Looking for a restroom, she wandered off around the side of the sagging building. It was good to stretch my legs. I wasn't aware of how cramped and stiff my body had become.

A family of expressionless Navajos lingered around a battered pickup truck. If they looked at us at all, they stared right past us and didn't acknowledge our presence. Yet they somehow seemed to notice everything that was happening. I didn't know that direct eye contact in their culture can be considered impolite. Feeling self-conscious and out of place, I looked off into the distance and watched lethargic winds nudge pink puffs of dust into the heavens. I felt like we were intruding in an alien world. Dad leaned under the hood of the Jeep, tugged on a fan belt, and began checking the oil and water.

After a moment, a short, stout lady wearing a long purple dress greeted us from the door. Another Indian wearing a black cowboy hat wandered over to the Jeep.

Dad grunted, "Fill 'er up, Skipper." Dad was always coming up with names for people he didn't know. Acknowledging the request, a weathered face nodded and then seemed to disappear under the wide-brimmed hat. As I listened to the labored squeaking and chugging of the gas pump, I wondered if it was going to break down before our gas tank was filled.

Inside there was a dirt floor covered with worn wooden planks. In the center of the room was a pot-bellied stove. Some colorful handwoven rugs were hanging on the wall. An old, oak display case with cracked glass contained some handcrafted jewelry and a few curio items. They primarily sold groceries and the kinds of things you would expect in a rural country store. I think there were some cooking utensils along with an assortment of Dutch ovens. On the far side of the store were a couple of saddles, bridles, and some simple rope halters. The smell of fresh-cut leather filled the dimly lit room. This would have been a great place to outfit our cabin back at the mill site.

While standing in front of a small electric fan and enjoying a cold drink, I became aware of two children standing next to the counter. They stood remarkably still. The girl was very small; the boy almost full grown. He was listening to the whispering from the girl I assumed was his sister. Although she avoided direct eye contact, her inquisitive eyes began watching me very closely. Eventually she inched her way over to me and essentially wanted to know why our vehicle was such an unusual color. A peaceful old man who wore a magnificent turquoise and silver bracelet had been monitoring the interchange. Holding back any sign of emotion, he told the little lady that maybe it had gotten sunburned. Then we all started laughing. Mom was just coming through the door and heard the comment. I think she laughed the most. After some short polite conversation Mom bought the two kids some half-melted ice cream bars.

The woman who had greeted us at the door called the young girl over to her and talked for a moment in the native dialect. I had never heard it before. It sounded exotic, mysterious, and beautiful. The little lady disappeared through the door and into the blinding sun and soon returned from the pickup with two simple beaded necklaces. She presented us with reciprocating gifts. The child couldn't have been more than six or seven years old. It was obvious she had made them herself and she was very proud of them. At the suggestion of her elder, she was giving us a gift in return for Mom's goodwill gesture. She had expended conscientious time and effort. All we had given was some pocket change for some refreshment that she might have been able to get for free.

Mom politely refused the gift. With a perplexed look on her face, the child glanced back at the woman behind the counter.

She presented her gifts again. Mom began searching her purse for some more pocket change. My mother had misunderstood the gesture. She thought the presented items were for sale. The proud lady who may have been a mother or an aunt began to stiffen. I felt a subtle sense of shame and uneasiness. What should have been a friendly exchange was turning into an insult. The little girl was looking confused and wounded.

Dad was paying the gas bill. I hadn't been aware of his presence. As he finished, he squatted down and began to carefully examine the gifts.

"I don't know, little darlin', that looks like some pretty fair workmanship. I don't know if I've ever seen anything so nice."

He was a bit patronizing but his intervention seemed well received. He stammered for a moment, then his eyes began to widen. He stood up and said, "I'm gonna have ta go out ta the Jeep and think this over. Be right back."

He rummaged around under the seat of the Jeep for a minute or two and then returned with an unblemished piece of quartz crystal. It had been picked up in some old mining dump while prospecting. Bright and cheerful eyes said it all. The trade was a resounding success. We had communicated. We had touched each other and it didn't cost a cent. Dad had a special knack for such things. About the time I thought I knew him, I always got another surprise.

It was good to stop at that little oasis and meet such kind and perceptive people. It was a place where Oscar would feel right at home.

We arrived in Gallup in the late afternoon. We met Grandmom and Granddad at a motel where they had paid for adjoining rooms. There was a lot of excitement. It was a happy time, a time of shrieks and hugs. We went to a restaurant where Mexican food was served.

The next day there seemed to be some controversy developing. There was a lot of discussion between Dad and Granddad about business. It was never clear what the business was but I knew it had to do with money. The "women and the kid" were sent across town to "do some shopping" so that "the men could talk."

We looked at a few shops and I think we "took in a museum." The abundance of Indians made Grandmother a bit nervous. We decided to cut our excursion short and have "a bite to eat." They wanted to sit and to continue their incessant talking because they had "a lot of catching up to do." I was restless and wanted to explore. Stepping outside, I was greeted by a pathetic man sprawled on the sidewalk and leaning against a rusting trash barrel. He was begging for money. The odor from him was putrid. He reeked of cheap wine. He may have been incontinent. I had never seen anything like that and for a moment I thought I might vomit.

It was truly a tragic sight. As tears formed in his eyes, I noticed my own eyes getting moist. I sat down next to him but was careful not to get too close. Granddad had given me some spending money. I held out the money to the wretched creature. He grabbed it and clumsily stuffed it into his shirt pocket. Then he grabbed my hand and pulled me close. I pulled away, but he continued to hang onto my arm.

"I know I'm just a no good drunk Indian. All my family is ashamed of me. Sometimes I think it would be better if I would just die."

He let go of my arm and wiped some slobber from his face and tried to stand. His eyes rolled back into his head. He collapsed, banging his head on the trash can.

After a moment or two the hollow eyes opened and he tried to pull himself back up. He stammered a bit and then said, "I can see you have a good heart. I too have a good heart, but it does me no good. Indians have a hard time in this world. Things are bad enough for us, but I have stolen from my family and now no one will trust me or help me."

He began muttering about some sacred artifact that an uncle had placed in his keeping. The withering little man had apparently sold the treasure and then spent the money on his latest binge. He told me that I should go to Zuni and see where the good Indians lived. He said he didn't want me to think that all Zunis were just "lazy drunken Indians."

The restaurant owner burst out of the door and apologized in an angry voice. Rescuing me, he made arrangements to dispose of my whimpering friend. In a few moments a police vehicle gathered him up and drove away. Grandmother was horrified. Mom looked concerned and took charge, taking us back to the motel. That night you could feel the ground gently shaking from mile-long freight trains that passed through the town. I wondered what had happened to my emaciated friend. I wondered where the Zunis lived. I found myself saying a prayer and hoping that an anguished soul might find some peace and forgiveness. When I had finished my prayer I found myself wondering who I was praying to. I found myself wondering why it seems that prayers are seldom answered.

The next afternoon Granddad decided to take the family to Zuni Pueblo. According to the pamphlet the desk clerk had given me, the Zunis had always been enterprising traders. They were especially known for their colorful and intricately crafted jewelry. As we rode along in the comfort of a large air-conditioned station wagon, I noticed that the landscape was becoming more interesting. There were occasional trees among the gently rolling hills. Shallow mesas floated by as if they were on a three-dimensional movie screen. Resting my head against the window, I watched the brown grass and gray-green sage turn into a blur. After a while I fell into a light sleep that was disturbed by an occasional bounce in the road.

Feeling the car slow down, I sat up and stretched. I observed a strip of green toward the right of the road where cottonwood trees were flourishing. We were approaching a hamlet of simple adobe and stone architecture. You could see glimpses of a slow-moving stream meandering toward the center of an adobe village. The car stopped just outside the pueblo in front of a building that sported a faded, hand-painted sign announcing that there was Indian jewelry for sale. On the other side of the door was a colorful painting of a large kachina that aroused my interest. We were assaulted by a large playful puppy as we climbed out of the car. He insisted on following me all the way inside the shop.

There was an abundance of finely-crafted jewelry fashioned from silver, turquoise, coral, jet, and shell. My grandparents were intrigued by the quality of the Zuni craftsmanship. After what seemed like hours of posturing and negotiation, they spent two or three hundred dollars. I too was very attracted to the jewelry, pottery, and kachina dolls. However, what they were spending seemed like a fortune. I remember thinking that in Telluride we were paying forty dollars a month for one of the nicest houses in town. They bought me a simple but exquisite silver ring that contained three pieces of turquoise and one piece of coral. Nevertheless, I was still quite attached to the simple beaded necklace that I continued to wear around my neck. My grandparents said they wanted me to have "something nice," so as an afterthought they bought me a bola tie that matched the ring.

Grandmother had become particularly attached to a piece of pottery that had supposedly come from a Hopi pueblo in Arizona. Granddad had grown weary of the game of negotiation and began to realize how much money he was spending. As they haggled between and among themselves, I went back outside and became engaged in some playful wrestling with the puppy that had greeted us when we arrived.

Suddenly, everything within me came to attention. The air was filled with mystery and power. Somewhere within the maze of adobe, a drum had begun to beat. It was as if I had discovered the beating of my own heart. My breath became deep and slow and the back of my neck and the top of my head began to tingle. Each beat of the drum was drawing me deeper and deeper into some kind of intense experience that my heart found familiar but my tantalized mind couldn't remember or comprehend.

The family was coming out of the trading post and was talking about the drumming. One of the Zuni proprietors was explaining that the Kachinas were dancing. He sensed my interest as I pressed for details. After a few questions, he suggested

that we would be welcome to attend. Grandmother looked a bit
nervous as she clutched her purse and newly acquired jewelry,
probably remembering the man on the sidewalk in Gallup. I began fielding some resistance about getting back to Gallup before
it got too late. I was surprised at my unusual sternness and per-
sistence. In a few moments one of the Zuni merchants turned
tour guide. Granddad and I followed him through the labyrinth
toward the walled plaza that was demanding my attention.

While Dad waited with Grandmother, we climbed onto an
adjacent roof. From there we watched the kachinas dance while
our Zuni host quietly instructed us on the meaning of the ceremony. This seemed routine for many of those who lived there.
For me, it had become a miraculous discovery. Although I didn't
have the words at that time, I now realize it was the first time I
had seen the power of pagan mythology coming alive. Through
the witnessing of ceremony and sacred community something
within me was being awakened and reclaimed. The knowledge of
the interconnectedness between the people, the earth, and the
sky had blossomed. The colors, the images, the movement and
sound propelled me into a gentle state of wonder and awe. It
might have even been bliss. This was something very special.
Something had stirred and blossomed in a way that would once
again reaffirm the quest for the ravens.

Mom had made an acquaintance with an Indian lady who
eventually brought the rest of the family to the plaza where she
explained the meaning of the ceremony. Some of the dancers
were her relatives. At the conclusion of our adventure we slowly
retraced our steps to the car. Driving back to Gallup that evening, the stars seemed to be brighter and more numerous; the
moon appeared to be larger and more luminous. It was good to
see how my family had been touched. The Zunis were generous
and insightful hosts. My mother had relaxed. My grandmother
was gushing with astonishment at all that had been seen. The
presence and the power of the ceremony lingered well into the
next day. But within forty-eight hours we had returned to
Telluride.

*   *   *   *   *

We were now living in a house that was located within half a block of the school. It was morning and the bell was pounding. At that time the belfry was still in use. Each morning about five minutes before the start of classes someone would begin pulling the rope and a rhythmic clang would echo through the valley, notifying the community that the doors were open and it was time to be in school.

I had become a rather late sleeper and sometimes I would use the five-minute chiming as an alarm clock. One particular morning I was already up and dressed, but still behind schedule. I bent over the bathroom sink and splashed water on my face and head. As I combed the excess water out of my hair, I noticed my mother standing behind me in the doorway. She seemed particularly agitated. I observed her eyes darting back and forth. She cleared her throat a couple of times, started pacing, and then mumbled, "I have to talk to you."

Setting my part with a small black comb, I glanced at the Busy Corner Pharmacy watch that Granddad had purchased for me during his last hunting trip. Completing the masterpiece of that special little curl, I became aware that time was running out. I groaned out an anguished whine, "Mom, you're making me late. I have to get going!"

Pointing her finger, she declared, "Now you just wait a minute, young man. This is important. It will only take a minute!"

I tried to ignore her, but I knew when Mom started pointing her finger that she was getting serious. Even if it wasn't really important, I knew she was immutably transfixed. Grabbing a Danish sweet roll for breakfast, I headed toward the back door. I knew it would be my last chance to duck the shrieking finger. Dad was already out of the house, probably having coffee at the Roma Cafe. I figured she had a message from him about a messy room or clinkers and ashes that needed to be hauled, or perhaps a lecture about feeding the dog.

As I opened the back door, she sternly grabbed me by the shoulder and I turned around. As she folded her arms across her chest, she looked at the floor and grimly stated, "We are going to move."

She said preparations had already begun. Pulling her bathrobe tightly around her waist, she released a defeated sigh and said it would be very soon. As I walked the two or three hundred feet to school, my mind kept ruminating about what she had said. Maybe I'd misunderstood. It seemed so unreal. The prospect of leaving the valley seemed like an idea that had nothing to do with what was going on in my life. An empty hollow feeling began to creep into my body and seized control of my mind.

It reminded me of the experience I'd had during the Cuban missile crisis. Late into the night I listened to the old Bendix radio in my upstairs room. There was a feeling of impending, inescapable disaster. There was a tangible vibrating energy of fear and panic. It permeated my entire being. At times my body would actually tremble from the intensity of the fear. My mind just hovered there listening in curious disbelief that at any minute atomic bombs might bathe the world in radioactive dissolution. My mind might be able to discount the news reports, but my body was telling me something ominous was on the verge of erupting.

I remember Dad coming home from the Elks Club where the men had been talking about the situation. He was very somber. All he said was that it looked like things could get real serious. He began to fumble with his hunting and fishing gear and then looked through the pantry. He went to bed early. Mom blended into the background and pretended not to be concerned about anything while she put away dishes that seemed to clank all by themselves.

In school, one of our teachers told us about the volunteer fire department's plan. A hasty inventory of the grocery store was taking place. In the event of an actual nuclear attack we were to gather up basic clothing, blankets, and food. Idarado Mining

Company offered their trucks. Everything of survival value would be stored in the mine. The entire population of the town would go underground into Ajax Mountain. There, under the supervision of our local officials, we would be assigned housing areas and rations.

There we would wait for clouds of radioactive dust that would drift in from the harbors and military installations of the West Coast. The class clown attempted to tease some of the girls, asking if they had ever eaten rats. No one laughed. Our teacher, a volunteer fireman, nervously fumbled with a dented Geiger counter, trying to see if it would react to the radium dial on his watch.

Acknowledging the tension in the room, we changed the subject. Our teacher shrugged his shoulders and said confidently, "It's in God's hands now."

We returned to our classwork, hoping it would all go away. Fortunately, it did go away. The crisis passed. A shaken world breathed a welcome sigh of relief and the potential for world calamity was soon eclipsed by the more mundane machinations of everyday activities.

But like the gentle haunting spirit of my first deer, the terror of the probability quietly lingers. Put aside for long periods of time, it sometimes leaks into my preconscious mind and hovers like a future prophecy or an unshakable ancient memory of a consummated event from another time, another age.

The idea that we were actually going to leave Telluride left me with that same kind of confusion and disbelief. Something inside me kept hoping that this crisis would fade and just go away. Yet I could clearly sense that the decision was very real. And this time the crisis did not pass.

I think Mom had a hard time with Telluride. It was a real love-hate relationship. The first house we lived in didn't have any electrical outlets. Lighting was installed by running parallel wires on painted rubber insulators. The circuits ran up the wall and across to the center of the ceiling. In the middle of each room was a single lightbulb. By screwing a special plug into the ceiling, you could retain the lightbulb and still have an overhead outlet. There was a lot of complaining about not being able to use the electric frying pan without blowing a fuse. Shaking her head, Mom claimed that the floors sagged so badly that she could pour water in the center of the floor and it would run downhill to all four corners of the room.

She made some friends who still ask about her. However, there were also some hurt feelings when the rumors started about how spoiled she was because she didn't even know how to use a wood-fired cookstove. Each time we moved to another house she got more electrical outlets. Eventually we rented a house with an electric stove and a coal stoker for heating. It was even regulated by a thermostat! The house was awfully expensive. It was the house that cost forty dollars a month. It was good not to have to chop all that wood. However, now I had to shovel coal into the bin twice a day when it was cold. The clinkers had to be removed daily. Sometimes the furnace would go out. Everything would have to be cleaned out and the gravel-sized coal would have to be re-lit using kindling.

It was too bad that she stopped making bread. She had mastered the wood-fired oven. Sometimes the loaves would be a little crispy on top, but that's just the way I liked them. Regardless of the ordeals she endured in Telluride, it gave her a lifetime of stories to tell.

★   ★   ★   ★   ★

One winter night some teenagers were racing cars through the icy streets. Someone lost control and a car crashed right through the corner of the living room. I had been sleeping downstairs next to the warmth of the wood-burning stove. I remember glass flying all over the room and thinking that there was an explosion or earthquake. As I realized that a car was wedged into the corner of the house, a teenage girl swung open the door, sprang from the car, and ran screaming through the house and out the backdoor. It was the event of the season. I remember standing outside in the lightly falling snow, wrapped in an old army blanket. The neighborhood women brought warm drinks and comforted me. The men laughed and teased each other while hanging canvas tarps over the huge opening in the corner of the house.

I remember the house on Oak Street where there was a hot water storage tank that sat right beside the kitchen stove. When you turned the valve, water would circulate through a lead pipe in the firebox. The heated water was then stored in the galvanized tank. When it got hot enough, you could go upstairs and have a hot bath in a huge free-standing galvanized bathtub.

One winter day the valve leading into the stove was left open. The water got a bit too hot and tremendous pressure built up in the system. There was an explosion. The pipe in the firebox had burst. There was soot, ashes, coals and, of course, water, all over the kitchen.

Mom was running around hysterically trying to mop up the steaming water and ashes that poured all over the linoleum floor. The sludge flowed into the pantry and down the steps to the dugout basement where wood and coal were stored. We didn't know where the water turnoff valve was located. Dad wasn't home, so we were on our own. Eventually, a county road maintenance worker showed up and saved the day.

The punch line of the story was that I was drilling holes in the floor with a brace and bit to let the water drain down into the basement. Mom grossly exaggerates the story. The drilling was only a suggestion. I still think it was a rather creative idea considering I was only eleven at the time.

All in all, I think she enjoyed her Telluride adventure but she was relieved when it was over. She never returned to Telluride. Having lived through hard times during the Great Depression, I think she preferred to watch from the sidelines and hoped to avoid any potential for hardship. I don't think she ever realized that difficulties and hardships are what create character and confidence. For me these challenges make my life real and worth living.

From her perspective, Mom had had enough challenges for a lifetime and was happy to leave. Our family, however, was poised upon the brink of a major challenge. The move was perhaps the beginning of the greatest challenge the family would ever face. Still, from my point of view, Mom's ominous words sounded just too incredible to be taken seriously.

I had finally gotten to the point where I was an asset to the basketball team. Starting out awkward and clumsy, it was good to know that a person could improve and actually get off the bench. I had struggled through my first attempts at dating and was beginning to make an amazing discovery. Some of the girls that I found attractive were also attracted to me.

I was playing an Hawaiian steel guitar with my friend Bob at the Sheridan Hotel. We were really terrible, but we were having fun. Sometimes people would dance to our dreary tunes in the nearly empty dining room. A couple of times we even got tips from lost tourists. Our roving music teacher once put together a New Year's Eve band that played at the Elks Club. I think anyone who could play an instrument was there. People were happy to have live music no matter how bad it was.

As a high school student, I now had my classes on the top floor of the school. We no longer had our entire grade together in one classroom with one teacher who instructed eight or nine students. Now we mixed freely with other grades and had several teachers. We had almost forty students in our high school. It was an exciting time. Astronaut John Glenn was orbiting the planet. It was a good thing the television booster tower was working. The whole school huddled around a black-and-white television set to watch history being made.

That summer I helped open up a collapsed portal of an old mine that had been buried under slide rock in Bridal Veil Basin. Gator, one of Oscar's brothers, got all excited when I pried a large piece of ore from the vein that was full of promising gold quartz. Dad let me drive the Jeep on the back roads. I was becoming a man. This was my town, my home; these were my people. I was a child of the mountain.

Dad became sullen and distant. He seemed to have trouble making eye contact. Mom claimed that we were leaving to get me into the "real world" and out of this "unwholesome environment." I didn't question or protest. I just listened and continued to concentrate on improving our basketball game for next week's game with the school in Ouray, a town on the other side of the mountain.

★ ★ ★ ★ ★

A week later I was laying in a large, cold bed in an old hotel in downtown Prescott, Arizona. Only the essential belongings had been gathered up and placed in the station wagon. Dad had driven the pink Jeep. It was hard to sleep. There were intermittent footsteps outside in the linoleum hallway. Sometimes you could hear someone coughing in the next room. Mom and Dad were in the other bed. Every so often you could hear Dad flip open his World War II Zippo cigarette lighter. When he sucked on the cigarette, the tip would bathe his face with a warm red glow. You could see the shadowed features of his face through the darkened room. You could see his empty eyes staring at the rotating fan that hung from the ceiling.

Dad could never make up his mind if his prospecting and mining interests were a business or a hobby. While he was trying to figure it out, his money ran out. There was nothing left to say. I could feel his confusion and pain. I wanted to give him a hug and tell him I understood, but the anguish he was going through seemed to be too personal for me to interrupt. So I told myself I was getting too old for childish hugs. Mom slept soundly; she was exhausted. She probably did most of the packing and storage. Sometime during the night I fell asleep. When I awoke we began a whole new life.

We ended up in Glendale, Arizona, a suburb of Phoenix. Granddad had once again become a pioneer. He had purchased a small house outside of Phoenix in a new retirement center called Sun City. He seemed very happy with it. I found it to be a very curious place. Transplanted palm trees towered over broad boulevards. Every so often the cracked sun-baked earth would be flooded in order to keep the grass within the medians from dying.

Old ladies in pastel-colored pantsuits and carrying pooper scoopers chased poodles. People's lawns were made of painted gravel. There was a finely-manicured golf course and a huge recreational center. Sometimes Granddad would drive to the corner convenience store in a golf cart. Granddad tried to teach me to play golf. The game didn't make much sense to me, but I appreciated his efforts and treasured our time together.

The summers were so hot that most of the retirees would leave and retreat to the Midwest until fall. Grandmom wasn't too pleased with her new home, but she loved her family. It was good for her to be close to her son again. I thought of Oscar sitting on his porch admiring the mountain and was glad he didn't have to live in this strange place.

Sometimes we would go fishing. We enjoyed trolling quietly along the banks of huge lakes under the brilliant blue skies of the Superstition Mountains. We tried hunting, but something was missing. It wasn't the same anymore. I think there was too much asphalt under our feet. We were beginning to feel like sportsmen, but we didn't discuss it. Dad's heart was no longer in the hunt. He just went through the motions and didn't care if we got a deer or not. Whenever someone would ask about the famous Lost Dutchman's Mine, Dad would shrug his shoulders and say he didn't think it ever existed. He would say it was just an old prospector's story.

Soon the mountain became a forgotten dream and a dim childhood memory. I made new friends, graduated from high school, and with a little help finally got my first car. Sometimes I'd cruise Central Avenue. Although somewhat conservative, I became a child of the sixties and embraced my generation. As memories of the mountain recessed into oblivion, I entered college at Flagstaff. Eventually, I became a reluctant but fiercely proud soldier snared into a poorly executed war, an experience that somehow brought me great pride and shame at the same time.

I watched the Southwest explode as hundreds of thousands and then millions of immigrants flocked to the Sun Belt. I became a grateful husband and a proud father. And always did I question and wonder what is true and what is the essence of it all. I searched many scriptures, both traditional and unconventional. Although I had a Master's degree, I was not a scholar, but by volume and weight the bulk of my possessions were books. The most treasured books were those that pointed to the footprints of those who had become committed and successful in the art of spiritual questing.

Somewhere within me remained a trusting child, sitting on a rock waiting for the validations of ravens sent from the Creator. In time I became tired of reading the records of dead prophets and missing messiahs and slowly began to seek living teachers and singing scriptures.

Chapter Four

The Way of the World

A s usual, I arrive a few minutes late. Rolling in between a security fence and the back of the administration building, I slide off my motorcycle and carefully lower the kickstand with the edge of my boot. I briefly look up at the sun and say goodbye to blue sky as I enter a concrete cavern that has seen no sunlight since the day it was built. Sauntering up to the sally port, it immediately becomes evident that some disgruntled inmate has once more clogged the sewage system. The fresh stench of human excrement has become a too common occurrence in an inadequate facility that has long been overcrowded.

The electrically operated steel-barred door squeals and moans as it acknowledges my presence and jerks open. I search my pocket for a little metal chip, which is a recycled, metal dog tag license with the number forty-four stamped on the back. Moving forward, I present it to a uniformed woman who nods at me through the control room window and places the chip on a Peg-Board. She immediately sounds off with, "The specialist is here!" Then she casually hands me my allotted set of heavy brass keys that we like to call andirons. She directs my attention to several written messages from the shift supervisor. As I move into the corridor, a second sliding door jerks open with a rattling gait and then slams behind me. Inserting a large brass key, I throw open the bolt of a third door and enter the main causeway of the Pima County Jail.

Immediately to the left are three small cells that are reserved for high security risk inmates. In this instance high security usually means that the inmate is a serious escape risk, has been charged with very violent crimes, or has an overwhelming propensity to get into major fights with staff or other residents. Some inmates earn all three of these qualifying distinctions. The location is within sight and sound of the shift supervisor's office. Response time to any serious disturbance is immediate.

Peering out of the food-slot door is a familiar face. Some see Mr. Fate (as I shall call him) as a very scary fellow. It is rumored that he may have murdered over a dozen people. That's probably a gross exaggeration, but you never know. He has been convicted of several crimes and is approaching two hundred years of prison time without parole. He is appealing some of his cases and other charges are pending. The inmate is frequently brought back from the Arizona State Prison system in order to go to the local court. Rumor has it that it would be too expensive and unnecessary to charge him with all the cases against him. And some of the charges are much harder to prosecute than others. However, officials want to be sure that this convict will never stalk our countryside again. In a few years he will be executed by electrocution.

Mr. Fate is allegedly a member of a well-known prison gang that has a reputation for extreme racism. This organization tends to be blamed for occasional injuries and fatalities among prisoners who get in their way. As I slosh through the sewage that had been coming from under his door, there is an immediate volley of threats and insults. The water and electricity to his cell have been turned off. It is blatantly obvious that Mr. Fate is having a bad day. He is hoping to be placed within the general population and is not pleased with his private room. His rage has been unleashed because he had hoped to pass some messages to other inmates regarding gang-related business.

Mr. Fate has been involved in numerous violent episodes while incarcerated. He has permanently injured one of our more experienced corrections officers. That officer subsequently retired from the profession. The inmate has tried to escape on several occasions and there is concern that he may try again. I recall one instance in which a routine search uncovered a handcuff key. The obvious talent and creativity that was displayed in the

almost perfect rendition was a bit unsettling. It had been carefully fashioned from the pliable metal tube that contained his
toothpaste. Now he has to place his forearms through the food
slot and be cuffed in the presence of two officers before his door
will be opened. When he comes out of his cell his ankles are immediately shackled and his hands are cuffed to a belly chain.
Some administrators seem to take it personally when he tries to
escape. Considering his circumstances, I would find it perplexing if he didn't try to escape.

An angry and distraught officer snarls sarcastically, "There
he is. Why don't you counsel *him*? He needs rehabilitating."

The officer turns to a crowd of amused and jeering onlookers.
Since his performance has been completed, he takes a bow and
prepares to make his exit. Accompanied by the casual jangling of
keys, the officer opens a gate and clomps down another hollow-
sounding hallway. You become aware of a hate-filled pair of
ice-blue eyes watching you with the precision of an electronic
scanner. The eyes issue a blatant challenge and begin to prepare a
response for whatever you might decide to do.

This was not a normal day, but neither was it all that unusual. Eventually, Mr. Fate released enough frustration and rage
that he regained his composure and was able to salvage a little of
his dignity. He spent several hours meticulously cleaning up his
cell. However, before the end of the shift, he once again became
agitated and attempted to dismantle the plumbing while sharing
his last cup of coffee with me—all over my shirt. Mr. Fate was a
very powerful person. He exuded the strength and volatility of a
man who no longer had anything to lose.

Mr. Fate is someone we should all become familiar with. He
is someone that we cannot continue to ignore. His numbers are
growing every day. We will eventually have to deal with him
whether we like it or not.

Fortunately, most people will never discover this hidden corrections world. The longer one lives in this microcosm, the more
the outside world becomes a fading memory. The little universe
can grow larger and larger in importance. It may seem to become

more and more real and begin to usurp all of one's talent and energy. Sometimes one can develop such a strong attachment to the subtle perversity, to the seductive interplay, that one is actually more comfortable in this artificial existence than in the original world from which we all come.

This is a microcosm of the larger universe that struggles with the same issues. It is a dynamic, living system that creates its own cultures, religions, nations, and racial issues. There are thriving clandestine operations, wars, alliances, and underground economies. In the midst of occasional revolutions, great leaders come and go. Empires rise and fall. One can even observe periods of relative enlightenment and renaissance. It even has its own internal prison system for those who can't seem to get along and follow the rules. It is called disciplinary and administrative isolation, and it comes complete with its own procedures for hearings, appeals, and even pardons. Pardons are especially useful when we run out of the one-person cells where the disruptive citizens are housed.

The guardians provide the arena and struggle to keep everything under control. But their leadership is an illusion for, in truth, the residents can overrun their keepers at any time. Fortunately, most of the inmates are not aware of their power. It was disheartening to me that so many found it hard to see that the real power structure often lay hidden in the shadows where quiet but intimidating looks and glances so often directed the drama. Much of one's attention was placed on the more visible characters who, in my eyes, were seldom more than easily manipulated, ignorant puppets.

Only occasionally did the puppets rebel and reveal their capacity for strength and creativity. Much of the true power went about its business unnoticed or begrudgingly denied. Again, I have often been astounded at the stark similarities between this little microcosm and the larger world that thrives just outside, past the steel doors. With some careful attention and a little patience, a person can discover a whole series of archetypical patterns.

I was selected along with four others to be employed as a corrections specialist. The facility was in the process of upgrading all aspects of its mission. A new state-of-the-art corrections center was in the planning stages. Meanwhile, we had to do the best we could with what we had.

We worked under the supervision of a classification committee of our peers and a core group of new corrections administrators. They had the authority to override anything we attempted. We would select security levels and assign new arrestees to housing units where we hoped the safety needs of the inmate and the security needs of the correctional facility would be adequately maintained. There was a continuous and wildly fluctuating stream of classification and reclassification requests. It was a world that had become burdened by its own overpopulation and lack of resources.

Many corrections officers had willingly donated weeks of overtime without pay based on the promise that they would someday be given some compensatory time off. Eventually, the training and budget requirements were worked out and the staff regained sufficient numbers to safely operate the facility. Meanwhile, there were times when we were simply not able to accept any more "guests." Then we would frantically search the records, hoping to identify a few pretrial inmates that might be released. When there was simply "no room in the inn," our lists were submitted to the judiciary while we waited for relief.

It was both a challenging and stressful time. It was a period of growth and change. This was an opportunity to test, redefine, and refine one's convictions and abilities. It was a time of intense political coups between and among semiretired, middle-aged servicemen and cops thrown in with a few ambitious young men, all attempting to scramble up the career ladder of bureaucratic success. It was a once-in-a-lifetime opportunity to make their mark and to secure a future as a corrections administrator. Some won and some lost. Some had other goals in mind.

I know we are supposed to call them correctional facilities. And they are supposed to be staffed by corrections personnel.

However, I'm not sure what we are correcting. Many people saw us as exacting vengeance. To me, it just looked like a place to put people who had become too malicious to ignore. I was always drawn to words like jail and jailer and tended to shun the more eloquent titles and polished terminology. For me, the old terminology was more accurate and precise.

One of my teachers was a thirty-year veteran employee of the corrections system. He was one who taught by his actions, not by endless chattering or rumination. Sometimes I would notice a slight auric glow around him as he stood leaning on the bars talking to the inmates down in "D-Run." He never professed to much spiritual conviction and he had a bit of a mischievous side. However, in an environment that could be a living hell, he was the kind of guy that you were glad to have around, regardless of which side of the bars you happened to be on. His relaxed, patient manner was not without occasional frustrated outbursts. He was the first to admit that he might need some time to mellow out. I never told him this because it seemed a bit mushy for a sterile corrections environment, but I would have been proud to have him as a father, brother, or son. We didn't socialize much outside of work. We probably would have argued about political and religious issues. However, we were good friends and we didn't have to talk about it to know it.

When day after day you look into the tragedy and agony of human perversity, it is hard to keep looking. It's easier to just keep walking down the run, avoiding the incessant rumble of inmate demands.

Which request is legitimate? Which inmate is conning you? Which task is yours? Which task belongs to someone else? During the days or weeks when the system is obviously not working, when things are breaking down and you see no improvement in sight, what is your personal responsibility? Are you looking into the tearing eyes of a desperate and repentant soul who needs your understanding, help, and compassion? Or is this just another vicious, manipulative psychopath running a scam on you so he can get to another tank and extort sexual favors and commissary items from the weaker predators? But there they are; their numbers and their demands incessantly multiplying. You must decide. What are you going to do?

You know that many of the quiet, almost invisible ones shrinking into the background may have the most legitimate need for your time and assistance. However, you may be reluctant to take them to the closet-sized office down the hall. You know there are troubles in the tank and you don't want to add to the general security problems. You don't want the tank leaders to become even more reactive and paranoid. They might suspect that the inmate has become an informant. If you get him a "snitch jacket," he could be in a lot of personal danger, especially if he ends up in state or federal prison.

As your eyes meet, you see terror. But is it only apprehension or a pleading for help? He is one of the younger ones. He is obviously scared and vulnerable and not too experienced, but he's perceptive enough to see how things work. Unfortunately, you don't have any place to put him that would be much safer.

You make the decision, unlock the door, and ask the inmate to come out of the tank. He ignores you, looks away, and pretends he doesn't hear you. You give him a stern directive and wonder if you are going to look weak and foolish because you might not be able to back up your demand. With a trembling voice he curses you and makes vulgar suggestions. You repeat your directive. You hope you don't end up in an escalating power struggle that would undermine your credibility and contribute to a growing lack of responsiveness to corrections personnel. Then he starts to come out. Someone glares at him and someone else moves forward to block his path.

To the amazement of his companions and himself, he pushes the inmate out of his way and tells him to mind his own business. He grabs a half pint of souring milk that has been laced with urine and hurls it in your direction. He blurts out that he'll come out when he feels like it and right now he doesn't feel like it. A gagging stench runs down the newly painted concrete wall. The "old guard" within the tank are impressed and a bit surprised. You see it on their faces. They know how hard they've been pushing this young punk. Perhaps he's on the way to becoming someone's involuntary girlfriend.

You see them thinking. "This kid has got guts. He isn't going to snitch on the wolves that have been harassing him. But he's a bit scared. He might freak out and hurt somebody. Maybe they should leave him alone. Looks like he'll work out all right."

They remember their first time behind bars. They laugh. For now, the tension is broken. Now he has another kind of "jacket." You hope he doesn't take it too seriously. He may develop a self-fulfilling reputation. The incident will be written up but, since you ducked and single cells are at a premium, there won't be much of a response.

As you wander deeper into the dim smoky maze, you wonder if next time it will be the kid who will take the role of predator. You glare and curse and try not to show how pleased you are with the results of your intervention. Your elder colleague was right. Sometimes you just need to let them call you a son-of-a-bitch so they can release a lot of their anger, fear, and apprehension; regain a sense of personal dignity; and make it through one more day.

Some of the jailers just don't understand you. And they let you know it.

"Why do you put up with these assholes? They're never going to change."

"They deserve what they get and more. You damn specialists are just stirring things up."

"The best way to take care of these animals is to make things so horrible that they'll straighten up and never come back."

"They got along just fine before you got here."

How did these caretakers of our aberrant brothers and sisters become so cold, so harsh? Were they always this way, or does this happen to a person out of self-defense?

Policemen sometimes have a hard time understanding the correctional setting. They get to dump the fruit of their labors into our cozy abyss. Cops can curse them and forget them. We can't forget them. We watch them, feed them, clothe them, and minister unto them. We are like babysitters. They depend upon us for everything. By virtue of the situation, we have to live with them. We are their servants, whether we want to admit it or not. We experience their every mood, their every outrage, their every concern, their every need. The faces may change but they never go away. They just keep multiplying. There are not enough jails and prisons in the world to house them. Eventually, we are going to have to deal with them, our wayward brothers and sisters. They are not going to simply vanish into cozy little concrete caverns.

There is something subtly perverse about standing in the way of someone's freedom. Most of these residents are obviously dangerous and harmful to our society, both collectively and individually. It is obvious that, although the massive economic drain of incarceration may not be the answer, we have not developed a viable alternative. But when you bar the door and remove rights from a person that you have not previously met, it becomes a direct assault toward a person who has personally done you no wrong. There is no way around it. You are the one who holds him in physical bondage.

We begin to rationalize and develop abstract generalizations about why we stay to take part in the drama. Escaping this often suppressed reality is very difficult. It frequently manifests itself in a growing tendency toward sarcasm with a touch of sadism that we seldom admit to ourselves.

After a while you begin to observe haunting similarities between the cagers and the caged. You wonder about those that don't acquire that revelation. You begin to count the cases of those whose crimes were so minor that they should have never been cast into this wretched pit. You begin to see how easy it could be for anyone to become caught in this seething travesty. Then you shake your head and realize that there are still some fundamental differences between "us" and "them" and you decide to read up some more on the Stockholm syndrome.

It is easier to become sarcastic and suspicious than to feel the anguish. You prefer to let yourself go numb and become unfeeling and uncaring; continually on guard, wary that "if the inmates don't get you, then the administration will." It is a natural process to become aloof for long periods of time and then suddenly overreactive. You begin to detest seeing the same old problems surface over and over again. You develop periodic migraine headaches. You've told this inmate five times that he can't get what he wants. He won't hear you. You stop trying to communicate. The corrections officer tells you the inmate's getting agitated. The officer says this guy is going to "go off" and it will be your fault if someone gets hurt because you won't do anything. The inmate needs more than you can give. Maybe he needs more than anyone can give. Actually, it's the inmate that needs to learn how to give. But he won't. So you fill out a form in triplicate and help escort him into isolation so no one has to deal with him anymore. At least not until the next shift.

After dinner you make another round through the tanks. You see that same corrections officer that was just lambasting you a little while ago for being some "dewy-eyed, liberal social worker." He gets a funny look on his face as you discover he has bent the rules a little bit and is helping that kid in C-3 make an extra phone call to his pregnant girlfriend.

The young man in C-3 acts very strong. He is strong. He is fond of flexing his barrio-acquired tattoos. He holds the phone tightly and tries to convince himself and the world around him that everything is going to be all right. The officer hangs up the phone and puts his hand on the kid's shoulder, guiding him back down the hall with a fatherly concern. As the inmate heads back to his steel bunk, he turns his head and wipes away the tears hoping no one will notice. From now on the old brown-shirted redneck can rant, rave, and bluster all he wants, but it won't do any good. You've caught him red-handed. You know that he cares. You both know you're caught in the same relentlessly painful rift.

Since that time, the new state-of-the-art complex has been completed. Looking back, it is sometimes hard to believe that such a place actually existed. Things were not always that intense and dramatic; much of the time things were downright boring. But sometimes they were more difficult than words can express. It was an excellent place to get to know yourself; to begin to understand others; to discover your humanity or the lack of it; to observe and to reflect upon the nature of your conscious and unconscious thinking, feeling, and doing. It was the tempering of the blade in the fire. It was a rich training ground for a householder who would become a pilgrim on a sacred path.

Chapter Five

The Struggle for Dharma

In the quest to make sense of it all, the spiritual studies continued. It was good to learn about sanghat and dharma at the Maha Deva Ashram near the university. I was exploring Kundalini Yoga with a lustful appetite. On occasion, I would rise at three in the morning and attend the morning spiritual practices of sadhana. It wasn't unusual to take in several yoga classes a week. I was enamored of what Yogi Bhajan was attempting to accomplish and ravenously consumed all the knowledge that my busy mind and schedule could handle. I treasured the lifestyle, but somehow could never quite make the commitment to become a Sikh. Somehow there was always a sense that my ultimate path would lie elsewhere. I found my wavering and lack of commitment to be a bit repulsive. However, no one else seemed to mind. It was the mission of the ashram to share knowledge, and I was there to learn. The dharma had an accredited drug program and I had served as a liaison to refer clients when I worked as a psychotherapist at Kino Community Hospital. Sometimes their yoga teachers would teach a few relaxation techniques to both patients and staff. It was a great way to enhance community understanding of yogic philosophy and provide access to an alternative substance abuse treatment program.

On my thirtieth birthday I decided to take my motorcycle into the Sonoran wilderness. There I met Swamiji gracefully walking through the flowering desert. He was a striking figure. A few silver threads were just beginning to appear within his thick beard. His long black hair, bronze skin, and pure white robes were the perfect picture of how a spiritual teacher was supposed to look.

Something immediately told me this was an old friend and he was to be my teacher.

I had already been intimately involved with the Maha Deva Ashram and it had much to offer. However, I felt an instantaneous drawing, knowing, and recognition that this is the one who should be given my attention and loyalty. This would be the one I would acknowledge, accept, and trust as I continued upon the spiritual quest. It seemed that there would be no purpose in seeking further when right before me was the living repository of wisdom that my aching soul demanded. To avoid this next obvious step was totally unthinkable.

It was the same kind of knowing that emerged when I first encountered my wife. She was my spouse long before we met. Upon seeing her, we knew we were to be married. The rest was just life-giving waters cascading down the hillside, notwithstanding an occasional mudslide from a raucous cloudburst. This is the kind of knowing that is so obvious that it can easily upstage an incredulous mind that becomes jealous and demands, after the fact, to seek confirmation of the appointment through logic, deduction, and dissertation.

Consequently, before too long I found myself engaging my highly trained and perceptive mind to make sure this was not going to be a mistake. After all, I was going to be prudent and would not be swept away by the emotionalism of the moment. I was not going to become just another dim-witted new age groupie. I am much too intelligent and sophisticated to become another cult victim of some sideshow guru.

After a year or so of sporadically attending his discourses, called satsang, I made my bid for immortality. Forcing suspect emotionalism and quasi-intuition into the background, I was determined to go ahead and do it right. I had decided that I would commit myself to doing the spiritual quest better than anyone had ever done it before.

It should be understood that I can be a most impeccable planner and formidable strategist. The mind is obviously a major part of the faculties of a human being and should not be discounted or casually dismissed. Some might rightfully argue that the mind is the true source of all human experience. Therefore, I had brilliantly constructed a concise list of essential questions that this holy man would undoubtedly be unable to wiggle out of, no matter how clever he may be. I would be able to get the information I wanted or show him to be of no use and merely an anachronistic cultural relic. The inquiring mind demanded to know. Who was this guy anyway? And how could he so profoundly capture my imagination and attention without even trying?

The first encounter was quite humbling. I was astounded to discover that he didn't particularly care whether I believed he was authentic or not. However, he was willing to be tested. The problem was that he was not sure whether or not I would be a suitable student or disciple. That was a real twist. Yeah, I'd read a few books, but a strong part of me just figured this guy would be interested in acquiring as many tithers as quickly as possible. It never occurred to me that a spiritual teacher wasn't required to accept whoever came through the door.

He sent me on my way, but politely suggested that I could return if there was continued interest. He even had the audacity to question my sincerity. Me, of all people! It was obvious that this wasn't working out. But I was no heathen. So I was cordial and respectful of his position. Then, I was out of there.

Fortunately, the attraction remained despite my best efforts to ignore it. The second attempt was much more difficult. It may have been the most terrifying experience of my life. It was dark, but the moon shone brightly. It was toward the end of an invitation-only conference where no one was turned away. I had carefully prepared a handwritten letter. It was a simple appreciation for what he represented and a request that I might be accepted into his sanghat. I sat quietly in my four-wheel drive International Scout for a moment and took a long deep breath.

Yes, it seemed clear that this was what I wanted to do. Stepping out of my vehicle, I strode toward the brightly lighted little house in the desert. It had been converted to a meeting place and hermitage for Swamiji. The closer I got, the slower I walked. I became increasingly riddled with panic and doubt. Had I lost my mind! I had heard all kinds of crazy stories. According to the books I had read and the several Eastern traditions I had studied, this man was to be as my god. In order to find my salvation, I would be following him totally and without question. Only through such a commitment and acknowledgment of his divinity would there be a chance at my redemption.

But what if he commanded me to give him all my money? What if he wanted me to give up my job and run his ashram? I had a family to support and a mortgage to pay. What if he decided to send my children to India for "special training"? What if he wanted to have sex with my wife? I'd heard stories about these new age guys. Some were actually revealed as lascivious perverts who enticed their victims under the auspices of practicing red tantric yoga. Such a commitment was hard to give. However, if I wasn't willing and able to do all that and more, then Swamiji would be right. I was not sincere, not worthy of the path of Gyana Yoga, or any other path for that matter.

Maybe this would be like Abraham in the Bible. It was just a test to see if a devotee who would be disciple is truly sincere. But if my act of faith were based on the idea that it was merely a testing, a ruse to demonstrate my conviction, then the exercise would be of no consequence. No, this thing required full commitment. There could be no reservations, no hedging, no second guesses or convenient insurance policies. Hell, it was just like he was Christ! Christ? What about Jesus?

Three times I had given my life to the Christian messiah. I was sincere. There was no question. I felt the presence. However, after a while the interest dwindled. The spirituality didn't dwindle but the interest in the church did. The spirit seemed real, but the wrapper seemed stifling, narrow, and superficial. If I was really saved, what was I doing here anyway? Wait a minute. I was saved. So whatever I did, as long as it was guided by the proper spirit, would be all right. After all, I'm just a hopeless sinner and I am saved by grace, not by my own actions. So there was no problem. Jesus had always been number one in my book. But my soul was longing for the rest of the story. I remembered a scripture that stated that in the last days we should be leery of false prophets, that many would come in his name saying he is the Christ and that a true believer shouldn't listen to them. They sure got that right. On every street corner there is someone claiming that this man from Galilee is the Christ. However, just what that means remains a mystery to those whose worldview begins and ends with Calvin and Wesley. Surely, God is bigger than all that. How come all the other civilizations were so stupid that they picked the wrong messiah while we were clever enough to pick the right one? A careful study of the "Holy Books" reveals a need by dozens of different scholars to rewrite and reselect and reinterpret over and over again. What happened? Didn't we get it right the first time? Why is there a need to continue to revise, recensor, and revise again? Maybe we just keep writing it until it comes out the way we want it to be.

The Dead Sea scrolls were really scary to some theologians and seekers. I found them fascinating and empowering. Historical Jesus seemed considerably different from the one who visited my church. Many people believe the name of Jesus is sacred and has tremendous spiritual power. They don't even know that he was never called Jesus; his name was Jeshua ben Joseph. We don't even seem to be able to get the name right.

And yet the spirit was there and it was strong. It was real. I was sincere. And there was a recognition that this new attraction was also authentic. I had come to the realization and conclusion that, despite my infantile machinations, anything big enough to be called God has got to be big enough to understand our dilemma and not hold it against us.

However, that was only my personal point of view. What if I was wrong? How does one know what one knows? Do we simply decide by an act of arrogant, belligerent faith, or do we somehow truly know? Is there another way? Some say that the only way you can know is by the guidance of the holy spirit. Well, I've felt the holy spirit. It guided me to Jesus and now it was guiding me to Swamiji!

But perhaps it was only the devil that was deluding me into believing it was the holy spirit. Perhaps these so-called holy men are personifications of the Antichrist. Perhaps Jesus was the real Antichrist and Swamiji was the one who was really trying to save me. The whole thing seemed to come down to who and what did I truly trust. My frazzled, tortured mind imploded. My frenzied, aching heart exploded in a flurry of quiet panic.

ENOUGH! Maybe I should just go back to my friends at the Maha Deva Ashram.

My feet felt like lead. My legs felt like rubber. I was perspiring as if I had run five miles. There I stood beneath the quiet desert sky where a host of radiant heavenly bodies were suggesting a multitude of ideas, feelings, and possibilities all stuck in one universe. There I stood, with my pathetic little note to Swamiji in hand, feeling defeated and foolish. I was revealed.

Whatever was going on, it was clear that I was a mess. I was an adult now, and there was no Mrs. Hancock to rescue me from the paradoxical universe with one big hug.

Now I was the little old reverend, pathetically shaking and unable to continue. I was facing my own crucifixion. Where on earth did all of this paralyzing gibberish come from? What was the source of this quagmire that was torturing my mind and inflaming my emotions? Where had I gotten the idea that I would ever be able to know everything or to even try? Where had I gotten the idea that I must make the perfect choice or face eternal oblivion? Where had this dark, vile curse that enshrouded my consciousness come from? I took another deep breath, then a deeper breath, and sat down right on the spot, feeling ignorant and humiliated.

Swamiji had required nothing of me. He welcomed me into his home and allowed me to hear what he had to say. He was a polite and gracious host. Whatever he was might not be clear to me, but it was obvious that I was becoming a lunatic and it was all in my own head. It was all my own doing.

I felt myself settling into the warm desert sand. The fears and contortions of my deluded psyche flowed out of me like the radiating heat that wafted up into the cool night air. I thought about removing my shoes. But I didn't. I just sat there. I continued to sit there and arrogantly wonder how one so wise and gifted could be reduced to such ridiculous circumstances. After all, I even had a Master's degree. I thought about laughing, but this was no laughing matter. This was an important time of crucial decision. It seemed that if I remained unable to make sense of this hurdle, my lifelong quest for spiritual truth would be grossly hampered, and perhaps permanently derailed.

From my seated position I rolled backward and allowed my body to collapse onto the ground. A few rocks and twigs painfully pushed into my back and legs, but it didn't matter. I listened to the serenade of crickets and the hum of distant traffic. A shooting star erupted out of the twinkling heavens, raced toward the horizon, and disappeared. I remember thinking that the meteor made a spectacular display but found myself saying, "So what does that mean? What does that have to do with anything?" I was still narcissistic enough to believe that some god force had put it there as a kind of omen or sign of what I was supposed to do.

Then I wondered if it was always so damned important for everything to have a precise meaning or a crystal clear answer. Perhaps sometimes things are just the way they are. The image of the Buddha drifted through my mind. I remembered the story of how he supposedly sat beneath a tree vowing not to move until he had achieved enlightenment. I briefly thought I might do that, but I knew it was only a wistful, willful fantasy. There had already been enough contrived willfulness for one evening.

Still, I sat, and sat, and sat some more. My mind halfheartedly continued to ponder, quietly whimpering from the depths of some dusty and abandoned well. What was true? Where was I to go? What was the meaning of it all? Was meaning a valid concept or only a sticky hurdle?

After a while I closed my eyes and began to pray to whatever god there might be that would wish me well. I prayed, not because I was worthy, but because the need was great. I confessed my weakness and my dependence. I acknowledged both my need and responsibility. I asked for patience and forgiveness. As I relaxed into the earth, a precious mantle of peace began to cover me. It comforted. It soothed. It hugged. My soul lapped up the nourishing nectar and was filled with a caressing gentleness. It was very welcome. It had been a long time. It seemed as if it was the peace that I had felt flowing from Mrs. Hancock. It was the peace I had seen in Oscar's eyes. It was the peace that had touched me when I made my solemn commitment to Jesus. It was splendid and complete. It was all that I had ever needed. I lay basking in the thick healing spirit. It was precious and intimate. In that moment it was all that had ever mattered.

I heard footsteps gently crunching into the desert sand. I sat up and opened my eyes. There, silhouetted by the rising moon, pausing for a moment upon the path, stood the Master! My heart leapt to my throat! It was Jesus, complete with long hair, beard, and robes. An instant later, I wondered if this was an apparition. As he brought his hands together in front of his chest and whispered, "Namaste," I realized it was *only* Swamiji. As I blinked my eyes, he drifted off into the darkness. Once again, I was left alone with the gentle presence.

Ever since that experience the Jeshua of my mind and culture has been liberated. No longer is His message imprisoned within one little black book. No longer would His message of love and forgiveness be molded into a finely credentialed system of social and political institutionalism. No longer would He be restricted to any time, place, or culture. No longer is He chained upon the cross of my limited perceptions and self-limiting machinations.

Of course, there is more to the story and perhaps one day I would find it. But for now the best course was to remain on the yogic path and follow this gentle guiding presence that had proven to be worthy of my trust.

There would be one more pilgrimage before the acknowledgment that Swamiji was to be Sat Guru. Frankly, it didn't make any difference if he accepted me or not. It was already clear what role he was destined to play in my quest for redemption. In time, he would continue to show me the machinations and structure of my mind: How to use it, and how to lose it. He would become a sanctified vessel through which I might become better acquainted with the divine. He would teach me contemplation and meditation. He would teach me secrets of my own heart and guide me through the mysteries of the creative forces. He became a door through which I would pass. He became a place from which I might recover my peace and discover the constant revelations of my soul. He would always be there, communing within the blissful presence.

Chapter Six

The Mountain Calls

I find myself remembering a quiet morning just off Old Spanish Trail in Tucson. A light drizzling rain had subsided just before the dawn. The morning desert air is filled with the smell of fresh sage. You can still see a few of the brighter stars through the remaining clouds. It is a good morning for jogging. The retreating shadows begin to reveal mesquite and palo verde trees. Somewhere in the distance a dog barks its challenge into the evaporating darkness, then listens for some familiar reply. As my feet pound down the path, a pink and yellow sunrise slowly emerges.

Where am I going? I'm really not sure. It just feels good to be alive; to be flowing across the landscape, feeling the blood pulsate through my body and monitoring the rhythmic ebb and flow of pure cleansing breath. I find myself chanting a delicate little mantra that had been acquired at the ashram. Paying attention to a complaining knee, my pace slows to a brisk walk as I approach a rustic open-air chapel located a few yards from the black asphalt bike trail that parallels the highway.

I don't remember the name on the sign. I believe it was a fundamentalist Christian group that had placed several rows of split-log seating facing a simple but alluring podium. It was surrounded by a low fence that employed a few rocks to complete its border. Toward the north are the Catalina Mountains, rising up out of the rolling hills of the flowering desert. It is a time when the polluted air isn't quite thick enough to obscure the view.

It was too primitive to be called a roadside chapel. The entrance was only fifty feet or so from the road. It was a place that might be used for Easter sunrise services provided that the congregation wasn't afraid of getting their feet dusty or muddy. I wouldn't be surprised to discover that by now it had become a parking lot for a large church complex. I found it an inspiring location for early morning meditation. A few times I even brought a small blanket and conducted my daily yoga routine in the midst of nature and in the presence of the rising sun.

Occasionally, a car would speed by on its way to join an increasing torrent of rush hour traffic. Sometimes a bicyclist or jogger would scamper along not even noticing my presence. After one meditation, I discovered an indignant woman standing before me; glaring intently, wanting to know what I was doing, but remaining too perplexed to ask.

She was a substantially overweight, heavily rouged lady who adorned her short silver-gray hair with a tinge of blue. My presence obviously made her feel uncomfortable. Perhaps she was a member of the congregation and felt that I was trespassing or defiling their sanctuary. There was some muttering about hippies as she retreated back into an aging but brightly polished luxury automobile. It was piloted by a stern looking gentleman in a dark shiny suit. He seemed impatient and irritable.

I began to wonder if I was inappropriately invading someone's private sanctum. The next moment I found myself thinking about how this rugged and beautiful place would surely be available for all those who would pray and meditate and seek a closer relationship with the creator. I would muse how this could be an opportunity to assert my right to practice my own particular path and give those with a more limited perspective an opportunity to deal with their own bigotry. Then I would think that I was being somewhat arrogant and observed that I had lost the purpose and focus that I had hoped to accomplish when my yogic practice session began.

The last time I paused at that location to meditate there was a raging sunset made more beautiful by a particularly putrid air inversion. An elderly gentleman who I had once seen exercising on an almost antique bicycle stopped and paused for a moment, staring at me with a sense of recognition. He then meandered over to one of the split log benches, sat down, and seemed to begin his own meditation. As I left the area, he looked at me and revealed a smile that seemed to hint that he knew something about me that I had long ago forgotten. He seemed to be a very curious fellow. After I left, I wondered if I should have stayed and chatted with him for a while.

But on this particular day something is very different. There is a subtle but definite uneasiness, a restlessness that will not be contained. There is an intensity that seems to override any ritualistic attempt at meditation. There is something stirring, something important and it is growing. It lies just out of reach of intellectual comprehension. It draws with a raw power that leaves me with an omen of profound and impending change.

I am sitting here, next to this historic Old Spanish Trail; this trail that has seen so much change brought by a multitude of conquistadors, explorers, adventurers, and pioneers over the past several hundred years. I find myself wondering what the original trailblazers would think if they were to make a return visit to this present age. How would they respond if they could see what has grown up next to their trail, the path to their hopes and dreams?

I find myself staring blankly into the awakening desert. As I try to pretend the restless feelings are not really there, I notice how native desert grasses, brush, and cactus are already reclaiming this little spot on the knoll that had been scoured and prepared as a place for organized worship. It seems absurd how we attempt to pave over and rearrange our earth in order to claim a place of worship, a place where we supposedly gain insight and give thanks for the Creator's universe of blessings.

This is a place that was perfectly beautiful all by itself without need of our propensity to rearrange and subdue it. Nature's wise and subtle way of forgiving this ignorant intrusion was already revealing itself in the healing of this well-intended but unnecessary scar. It is as a sermon prompting me to look into earth in a way that has been obscured and hidden by some invisible veil.

I feel like I am unraveling, struggling to regain my orderly routine. During morning meditation, I sometimes find myself surrounded by fluttering groves of aspen trees, feeling wind in my face, the earth beneath my feet. I am standing upon the mountains of Telluride, the home of my youth. This is not one of those trendy guided visualizations. This is the real thing.

Somehow I can feel the mountain calling to me. It reaches deep into my soul and touches things never before experienced, or perhaps things long forgotten. Images begin to manifest. I begin dreaming while I'm awake. The presence of the promontory reaches deep, promoting a growing sense of awareness. It is a sense of awareness accompanied by a pleading urgency.

A few days ago, it became so alluring that during the afternoon, I found myself driving to the airport, credit card in hand, wondering how much it would cost to get to Telluride. Although a visit might be helpful, a move would be unthinkable. It would be too irrational, too irresponsible, too expensive to consider. My life and career were here in southern Arizona.

Once again, I am in turmoil. Although reluctant, I know things are about to change, with or without my consent. Something demands that the move be made.

I've spent nineteen years of education culminating into a career in the counseling trade. I've worked several years in the mental health unit at Kino and the old Pima County Community Hospital. I've been a substance abuse counselor and a corrections specialist. I've seen mental illness: hallucinations, delusions, illusions, thought disorders, a multitude of disorders and syndromes, intellectualizations and rationalizations of all kinds. I've seen madness up close; real close.

I've spent months in Virginia Beach, Virginia studying the psychic readings of Edgar Cayce. I've chased enough psychics to know something about mediums and channeling. I've sported an interest in extrasensory perception and have sought out personal "readings" in my sporadic quest to uncover mystical truths. I've sought out experts like Dr. Rex Stanford at the University of Virginia's Department of Parapsychology. I've talked with people who finance expeditions to look for the lost civilization of Atlantis. I've chatted with people like Lynn Schroeder and Sheila Ostrander when they returned with their book, *Psychic Discoveries Behind the Iron Curtain*. I've studied, looked, visited, and diligently practiced yoga asanas and thoroughly read the *King James Bible* several times.

There have been times when there were interesting coincidences or vaguely familiar sensations. But this is different. This is not philosophical, theoretical, or abstract. This is strong; this is alive and real. Something is happening to me. Yet, I am in control. I am here. I am functioning and capable; a dedicated, hardworking, young family man with a very special wife, two energetic young children, and an aging mother-in-law.

I remembered some of the things I had been told about my life purpose from a local psychic. That was interesting. However, I didn't recall anything like this. Either I'm going crazy or something very revolutionary is upon me. It is time to seek counsel. It is time to seek guidance from someone with the appropriate knowledge and background for such things.

Throwing a leg over my motorcycle, I cross the urban tundra and ride deep into the Sonoran desert to seek an impromptu audience with Swamiji. It was fortunate that he was in residence and willing to meet with me. The road to the hermitage was just a rutted, sandy path winding across the desert toward a modest home. I once again found him meandering through the creosote and cactus, replete with long white flowing robes. His attendant was very protective and concerned that I would rudely interrupt her master's solitude. She wanted to ensure that he would be honored with the reverence that his stature and culture requires.

As our eyes meet, a comforting smile says it all. It appears that he was expecting me. It is easy to assume or fantasize such things. However, experience has proven that sometimes this knowing can be true. I could feel his drawing presence when I was hastily dashing through the traffic. The guidance was there and it was time to make use of it. Whether the assistance that was manifesting through this Eastern teacher was from Jesus,

Yahweh, Allah, Buddha or a mere reflection of some higher self, the attraction was as clear as it gets. I was thirsty and here was the well. It was time to drink and I was ready to drink all of it.

As he waved me forward and invited me into the ashram, all the tension and restlessness collapsed. I watched myself becoming peaceful and centered. Questions vanished and answers became irrelevant. There was nothing to say, nothing to be, and nothing to do. I have been here before. This is a typical phenomenon that happens when a devotee approaches those who have attained the path. It is comforting to have the chakras calmed and metaphorically to have a pacifier shoved into your third eye. However, I also knew that when I left the serene presence, the restlessness would return. So I pressed the issue as best I could, even though I knew it would be somewhat destructive to the emerging serenity.

I'm amazed about how he does it. As usual, he does everything right. He never seems to forget. Because of that, he enables others to remember. He made no decisions for me, just asked a few clarifying questions, focusing on the possible choices, revealing the one choice that is made over and over again until the time of completion.

There was a validation that whatever experience might be coming it could only serve to bring the opportunity to fulfill one's destiny, to learn and to grow. I was reminded that, properly understood, it is not possible to make a wrong decision. Error only serves to provide the perspective to define what is true by discovering what is not true. The strength and force of the restless energies that were welling up and spilling over into the conscious mind were only as an indication that a great learning was about to take place. My uneasiness was once again a reflection of my lack of understanding and trust.

There is often fear or resistance when major changes are on the horizon. Sometimes, there is a clamoring to accelerate or force something to happen too quickly, before it is ripe; or to attempt to experience it more fully than the current process allows. However, if one's feet are firmly on the path and the lessons are being learned, the reluctance eventually gives way to acceptance. Once again, through grace, the obvious next step on my journey was being revealed and acknowledged.

I must admit that this one has never lied to me or sent me toward unfertile ground. In accordance with the tradition, I was reminded that, no matter how much instruction is given and no matter how much knowledge is imparted, in the end one will always have to go within and take the last trembling steps alone. All the assistance in the universe is but a tool to help one find and claim the individualized path of one's own personal destiny. What he gave me was a sense of peace and confidence. He provided an arena within which to trust my intuition and to test my discernment.

Forsaking the day's work, I headed for the high ground and rode my bike up the Catalina Highway into the mountains northeast of the city. I left the road behind and followed a small dirt pathway until I discovered a quiet secluded place overlooking the hazy Tucson valley. Removing my helmet, I tugged briefly at my long ragged beard, pulled the rubber band from my ponytail, and shook loose the long bushy hair that cascaded halfway down my back. At work it had become a bit controversial. I had never intended to make it an issue. Somehow it seemed a natural outgrowth of a yogic lifestyle. It seemed as natural as breathing.

Seated upon a large rock, I draped an old gray Army blanket around my shoulders and allowed my body, mind, and soul to search for direction. I had never felt more free and alive. I believe I discovered for the first time what it means to be a yogi. Sitting quietly, being cradled by the beauty and solitude of the wilderness, I was filled with the familiar peace. Perhaps it was not enlightenment, but it would do for the time being.

All was well. There was a choice. Something unseen and very connected to the essence of my being was asking me to uproot everything and make a pilgrimage. However, the choice was mine. No voices, no delusions, no antiquated belief systems; just a clear undeniable realization that exciting and challenging times were upon my horizon.

However, it was hard to know how to proceed. The job was becoming a career. We worked hard and planned well. We were buying a few acres of ranch land near Arivaca. We were buying four houses; three were rented. Assets were appreciating due to community growth and appreciation fueled by inflation. There was some cash but not much. Our material assets would have to be sacrificed in order to successfully move a young family into a budding mountain resort.

Fortunately, it was a good marriage. We had listened to our hearts and planned with our minds. Although there are always cycles within relationships, this one has always been based on an overriding acceptance of the primary importance of spiritual questing. My wife was not a novice in such matters. Replete with the experiences of her own path; her pilgrimage once took her deep into the jungles of Guatemala in quest of a Mayan vision.

However, it seemed that I had gone as far as I could go. Although the choice was clear, I was hedging. I could easily make the choice for myself. But how do you make such choices for your children? My father had already shown me how difficult life could become without prudent financial planning. But he had also shown me what happens when you lose your dream.

*　*　*　*　*

One evening we were returning home from a movie. It was a cool spring night. We lived at the edge of the city. The tires crunched through fresh gravel in the driveway. We sat for a few moments in the car enjoying the moment. With an appreciated absence of street lights we were wistfully focused on the cloudless star-filled sky. After some casual conversation we began to meditate. I could feel a growing sense of intimate presence.

I began to see waves of shimmering energy disrupting my visual acuity. The shimmering sensation turned to a partially transparent veil of radiant light. Blinking my eyes, I looked towards my wife who seemed to be a blur of translucent energy. Slowly, from out of her mouth I heard an unfamiliar voice which said, "When the earth comes round twice; His torch shall blaze in the skies."

The intensity subsided for a moment. We regained our faculties and went into our modest slump block home. My wife was channeling. So-called psychic readings had begun to manifest through her. We were excited. We were awestruck. We were filled with apprehension and questions.

We thought we had grown past such primitive kinds of experiences. Then we were given a greeting and were told that this was as the opening, and a new beginning. This was supposedly a time when a group of over eight hundred souls were simultaneously coming into this level of ability and awareness. The "Source," as it was called, was coming "to comfort and to guide." We were given some instructions on how to make the channel more comfortable, to make the opening easier. Then we were told, "Go to the mountain."

Later, we were instructed to go outside and look up into the heavens. Several thousand feet above our neighborhood we watched the formation of a large circular cloud. It appeared in a sky that had been cloudless just a few minutes before. We were given the admonition, "Lest ye doubt."

We were on our way to the sacred promontory.

Chapter Seven

Home Again

While yawning breezes swell through dancing aspen leaves, long slender tufts of wild wheat grass playfully caress the side of my face. There I lay, sprawled across the ground, entertained by lazy drifting clouds, my body nestled gently into soft yielding earth carpeted with thickly matted green grass. This had always been a special place.

It is an easy thirty-minute walk from the valley floor. This is borderland. You can watch the mundane activity of the people in the valley while remaining secluded and undisturbed. Proceeding from this point, the winding trails that reach deep into the high mountain basins become obscured by magical forests. It is one of the last areas to turn golden orange in the fall. It is one of the first places to become green in the spring. If you listen carefully, you can hear the muffled gurgle of hidden water that flows just under the surface of the ground. Staring through the white mists and up into the azure sky, I realize I had forgotten what a clean sky was supposed to look like. It was good to be home. I had forgotten much, but I was remembering.

Early that morning I had awakened from a marvelously vivid dream. It seemed that a part of me was still in some kind of dreaming place. The vision had been bright and clear. The vibrant colors, images, and feelings of the dream seemed alive and real. My usual waking state was dull and inhibiting by comparison. Darting high across the face of the earth, covering hundreds of miles and millenniums of time in just a few moments, I relived the primal creation.

Possessing nothing but consciousness, we plunged deeply into ripe moaning earth. Shocked and startled by the incredible denseness, we emerged dancing from creation's cauldron. Sporadic bursts of purifying, cauterizing fire erupted with the intermittent shuddering and reshuffling of surface plates. Glowing granite waves stretched high into the heavens, twisting, writhing, belching forth gigantic blankets of ash, fire, and steam, bearing witness to our mischievous excavations. The earth groaned and shook uncontrollably in great harmonic waves of convulsive grinding that rippled around the planet. Between the throbbing upheavals, eons of rhythmic seasons brought the crowning purity of silent snow, feeding the green goddess, burgeoning forth with an endless tapestry of fertile and adventurous life. Occasional cycles of restless ice meandered across the face of the earth.

We were here; touching, feeling, embracing, emerging through the sacred womb that became our soul's birthplace; lunging into the earthly pilgrimage. We were alive; struggling within the mineral elements, evolving within the plant kingdoms, listening and watching within the spirits that began the animation of the great animal clans, becoming entrapped and mesmerized within our own clumsy experiments until grace wrapped our souls within physical bodies of our own so that we could experience, learn, and grow within this wondrous place. Words have so little power in the presence of experiences such as these.

The Source claimed that the conscious mind was recalling how we had first come to this place after the primal separation from the Godhead. It was as if a hidden ripple within the fabric of the soul's consciousness had been released. It was an internal record of our descent into this plane of existence. When I inquired further regarding this experience, I was told, "You have already remembered what you need to know."

This Source seemed to be providing all the usual revelations that have come through the many channels of this age and time. There was a validation that souls return to earth for successive experiences to ultimately reclaim their relationship with their Creator. Soul seed was strewn throughout the cosmos long ago.

As sprouting souls learn, experience, and grow, they become ripe with the purpose of their creation. The final harvesting and completion of the cycle is supposed to result in great joy and accomplishment. It is the reason human beings come into existence.

The Source was giving us recommendations on diet, and explanations on why this channeling experience was coming into our lives. There was the consistent theme that we were living not just on the brink of a so-called "New Age," but rather a culmination of several previous ages upon the earth. There was confirmation that the planet was entering an extremely difficult time of crucifixion. It was explained that the process could be a gentle evolution or a painful wrenching devastation.

There is an urgent, almost desperate plea to turn back to sacred ways before the potential for widespread calamity becomes inevitable. There seemed to be agreement with most other channels that the world as we know it is upon a precipice of irrevokable political and social change.

Prophecies were confirmed and expanded regarding the increased propensity toward massive earthquakes in California, the Northwest, the Great Lakes region, New York City and throughout the world. Catastrophic geological upheavals of an unprecedented scale would become increasingly destructive during the next few decades.

At some point there is the possibility of losing one- to two-thirds of the planet's population through war, disease, famine, and astronomical influences that may result in polar shifting. The American continents will become reshaped. Much of Europe will become submerged and India will be rent from the Asian continent. Japan may slide off its continental shelf. Ancient lands will begin rising from the sea. We were cautioned that this would not be as one single cataclysmic event, but rather an ever quickening evolution that will take several generations.

One of the greatest dangers is evidenced in the indiscriminate way that some of our governments and scientists have experimented with biochemical forces. It has been made clear that they don't sufficiently understand the implications of their tampering. They have no appropriate ways of controlling their mistakes. It is stated that, in their arrogance and quest for power and dominion, they are unbalancing the natural ecosystem in ways that may prove to be the gravest error of all.

We tend to see ourselves at the height of civilization, reveling in our great knowledge and wisdom. We bask in a seemingly endless array of miraculous technological accomplishments. We eagerly await an onslaught of even more seductive technology looming upon the horizon. However, this Source tells us that the history of human beings on this planet should be recorded not in thousands of years, but in hundreds of thousands of years. This Source tells us that we are not the most technologically advanced civilization that has ever existed.

Civilizations much greater than this one have been obliterated from the face of the earth. Although the remnants are there for those who have an eye to see, we usually have a hard time recognizing them because of our shortsighted perception of how long human beings have been on this earth. Our peoples have forgotten how inhospitable things can become when the delicate balance is defiled.

From the vantage point of this Source we are seen as awash in a sea of ignorance, poised upon calamity of a scale that has never before been seen upon this planet. It doesn't happen suddenly, all at once. It will take many generations to navigate the treacherous and painful path that will eventually lead us through the coming dark ages and return us to the always present and healing forces.

Although there may be many similarities, each individual path will be a little different. Many people will at first seem to be relatively untouched by this evolving age of impending revolution. Some may welcome and grow with the challenges. Some may be crushed by them. The various archetypical patterns will be played out within the lives of individuals, families, clans, tribes, and nations, as well as the planet itself.

Meanwhile, the seeds of new life are already being planted, ready to burst through the dark winter, to ignite a long awaited age of redemption. However, before the time of the resurrection there must come this time of cleansing and crucifixion.

It was to be understood that these are natural periodic cycles. These patterns were established at the time of creation. It is all a part of the great pilgrimage. This was the general message of this phenomenon that simply called itself the "Source."

Initially, the reality of this new partner in our lives that calls itself the Source was a bit perplexing. We thought we had graduated past the elementary stages of channeling and psychics. We were working on ourselves. We no longer had more than a passing interest in these interesting but unvalidated and unseen mentors. No matter how interesting or inspiring the source of a psychic channel might be, in the end it's just another source of information. You have to make a choice: to believe or not to believe; or to just pick and choose what makes sense to you based upon whatever wisdom you are able to employ.

In the end, people have to come to their own place of integration within themselves. Only through the privacy of one's own personal sanctuary does one truly meet their God, find their salvation, or become illumined. However, if the information we were getting was true, it seemed there was a responsibility to allow others to share in it, and to allow them to have the opportunity to come to their own conclusions.

I began recording every word that was uttered out of the mouth of the channel. It was our hope to make a record to be distributed to people who had an interest in such things. There was the uneasiness of what other people might think of a family was involved in such strange goings-on. What effect would there be on the children, employment, and friendships? We determined that personalities were not the issue. In fact, the personalities can create unnecessary problems. We would focus on documenting the information and creating avenues to share it. However, the Source had other plans.

This was not a source that would spend the channel's time giving hundreds or thousands of personal "readings" for a small fee. It would not make itself available at our whim. This Source was not particularly concerned with answering questions just because we would ask them. "When the time was right" it would present information. That which was coming through this channel spoke with a sense of authority and would come to its own conclusions about how and when things would be done.

Eventually, we began to recognize that most people were more interested in knowing a psychic channel than in hearing what the Source had to say or in responding to its message. We came to realize that the essential message was not necessarily unique. However, it was time to hear it again. This time we were participants, not merely curious observers.

This Source had a whole different approach than what we had previously seen. There were sometimes weeks or months when there would be little or no contact. We were told that there had been an ever increasing number of channels for several decades, that there was an abundance of information, some of it very accurate, some of it misunderstood, some of it falsified for selfish purposes. Some information has not been published or popularly circulated. Some of it is merely self-deluded fantasy.

This era of channeling was described as a time to introduce new ideas and concepts into this particular age and culture. It was a process of divine intervention that would provide some conscious understanding of what the ancient teachings were about and to provide some understanding of what is about to descend upon our world. This was a time to inspire the intellect and to make the will more pliable and able to consider other possibilities. This channeling is a technique that has supposedly been used in other times and other places.

However, the time had now come to get serious. The time for parlor games was over. This Source presented itself as a guide that would allow us to consider and discover our own unmanifest potentials and talents. The time was coming for the development of personal knowledge, direct knowledge, knowledge that doesn't require running to books and channels, knowing that comes with the authority of one's own experience, knowing that comes from walking with spirit that is holy. We were also warned that a time was coming when once again channels, seers, and prophets might be ostracized, condemned, and attacked by a new age of Pharisees capable of developing new versions of the witch hunt.

We had built our Telluride home with a loft that featured an east-facing window. This was our sadhana room—a place to practice yoga, pray, chant, meditate, and sometimes to receive readings. Sometimes it was used for a special gathering or to mediate a family conflict.

In the morning, the sun would rise over Ajax Mountain and come streaming through the window into our version of a kiva. I had placed a crystal in the window that had been selected by the channel. Refracting the sun's rays, it created a brilliant and repetitive array of rainbows upon the white walls of the room.

One morning during meditation, we were given instructions to take a trip through Northern New Mexico. We were to stop at many sites along the way. It seemed that this pilgrimage, including stops, would take about two weeks. Within twenty-four hours we were packed and traveling over Lizard Head Pass.

The Source was becoming fond of taking us to places where we could find markings from the pilgrimages of the ancient Indians, conquistadors, explorers, and pioneers. It liked to have us go in different directions, depending on the seasons. After several stops, we found ourselves at a location within twelve to fifteen miles of El Morro in New Mexico. The exact location will not be given due to obvious concerns regarding the tendency for desecration and pillaging of sacred sites.

After driving some distance off the main road, we were directed to stop and get out. Soon we were walking along a narrow, dusty path that was sometimes hard to follow. We climbed to the top of a small, rocky mesa where there were some unexcavated ruins. We saw some disturbed ground where people had been digging, probably searching for artifacts; perhaps they had been anthropologists. In the center of this little mesa was an oval-shaped valley that measured several hundred feet across. In the center was a spire that reached close to the same level as the rim that encircled it. Toward one direction was an expansive opening that was the same elevation as the plane below. We sat for a while, rested and enjoyed the view. Then the Source told us a most remarkable story.

I had already known that the Hopi people believe in a mythology of ancestral migration. According to their particular teachings, waves of people were sent out in the four directions. After a period of travel, the groups would stop and build new communities. Several generations later, a few might be called upon to continue the migration and leave other members of the clan behind. Their mission was to search, learn, and populate the earth.

In this manner the clans would wander across the earth, leaving behind many evolving societies and nations. A core group of the clan would eventually be called to return to the original home of their ancestors and complete the process of the circular migrations.

We were standing next to remnants of a shelter that was supposedly built upon ruins that were constructed several thousand years earlier. Native people consider it to be a sacred place, but much of its history has supposedly been forgotten. According to the Source, the people who migrated south began their journey in a time more ancient than most modern people would be willing to believe. It was claimed that the migrations began several hundred thousand years ago and lasted up until a few thousand years ago. To the Hopi people, Orabi, within the Four Corners area, is seen as the center of the earth, the place where all the migrations began.

Over time, some of these waves of migration evolved into cultures such as the Aztec, Maya, and Inca. Sometimes these migrations would meet and commingle with other cultures also on generational pilgrimages of their own. Throughout the millennia, the memory of their origin was usually handed down through stories and myths, and eventually forgotten by the general population.

This site was described as a place of rendezvous, a homing beacon where remnants of the migrating clans would return.

The last return supposedly occurred around nine thousand years ago. A group of people began their return from an area that later became known as the Incan Empire. It took several thousand years for the people to complete the entire journey. The returning remnants were guided by priests or shaman who were inspired by arcane teachings that were handed down through the ages. Sometimes there would be visions, intuition and assistance from this thing called the Source. The people that last returned to this location became known as the Zuni.

As the story goes, they originally attempted to reunite with their tribe of origin, the Hopi. However, over the millennia their ways had changed. Their mythology and ceremonies evolved a little differently. The Hopi elders were concerned that this might be a lost or wayward clan and that some of these customs were too far removed from the teachings that these Hopi believed to be true. The Source claims there was much discussion and anguish over this issue.

The Source indicated that there could have been some divine intervention to convince the appropriate elders of the validity of the returning clan's claims. However, this is not the way it was chosen to be done. It is ofttimes best for people to reach into their own sacred knowing in order to decide for themselves how things should be done. Eventually, it was agreed that this group would remain separate from the people at Oraibi. Accordingly, the Zunis reclaimed and resettled a portion of the land of their ancestors and became a welcome addition to the flourishing pueblo cultures.

The amazing part of this story is how the people returned. You see, there were supposedly three groups of people who arrived at the same place at the same time, each group being told that the other two groups would be there when they arrived. Beneath the floor of this large natural kiva are ancient artifacts left from the time of their return, their habitation and celebration. It is even claimed that there are records of teachings, migrations, and pilgrimages stretching back throughout the ancient millennia.

There are many places of records, which someday may be revealed when the right combination of people return with the right kind of intentions. We were told that in time ceremonies will once again be conducted within this ancient earth kiva. We were told that this was a place of celebration, joining, and harmony. We were told that there were many others waiting for the continuation and completion of their own sacred journeys. There are supposedly many sacred places rich with the power of remembering.

It was an amazing story. Perhaps it is mythology. Perhaps it is reality. Perhaps it is both. One thing is certain, our experiences with this Source were beginning to make me believe that such things might be possible.

In the next step of the journey we were taken on dozens of pilgrimages all over the Western United States; some very far, some right in our backyard. We visited countless ruins, communities, and sacred places. We were being offered an hands-on opportunity to begin our own pilgrimage, to explore firsthand the teachings of the land and the teachings of the people. And always there was the common theme of reviving and acknowledging the ancient and intimate connection with sacred land. Though I didn't know it at the time, the Source was inviting us to begin a quest to rediscover the history of our own ancient womb.

Chapter Eight

Invitations and Initiations

Swamiji sent word that I might ask for initiation. He had just returned from a trip to India. I found him within the mountains. He was slowly showing me the nature and structure of the mind, and revealing the power of a trusting heart. He was teaching me to meditate and was allowing me to discover a cleverly hidden place that is always alive and shining.

It was a quiet but intense afternoon. The ceremony was simple, subtle, and powerful. First we politely chatted. Then he reached deep within me and called forth an ancient mantra. I remember hearing a muffled rumbling of thunder that slowly echoed through the distant clouds. As he commissioned the sacred sound, I repeated it out loud as I had been instructed. With his head tilted slightly back and to one side, Swamiji watched to see, to listen, to be sure it was done just right. I repeated it again and again. He leaned forward and nodded, displaying his approval.

Guruji also recognized my spiritual name during the process of initiation. It is an ancient term that supposedly describes the essence of this soul's nature and mission. It was originally suggested by one who claims to be the last White Mahan Tantric. Three seasons before, it had been confirmed by the Source as being accurate and suitable for such an occasion. Now being sanctioned by Guruji, it was complete. The event was not only a culmination but also became another beginning.

Somewhere during our time together there began a soft healing rain. When it came time to leave, I bowed before him, cupped my hands, and lifted them over my head for a final blessing. He sprang to his feet, rummaged through his pantry, and presented me with an appropriate prashad. As I watched his contented bright eyes, I could feel the gentle presence of what I had been taught to call Jesus. The maturing Jesus of my youth was pleased, very pleased, and no one needed to tell me it was so. Jeshua Ben Joseph wrapped me within the blessing of my Sadh Guru and became the breath within my breath. Later in the day, after the dry thirsty ground had drunk its fill, a cool refreshing mist rose up from moist and fragrant earth. For a while it gently caressed the greening countryside, then was absorbed back into the heavens from which it had come. And, once again, life was rich and full.

It had been another miraculous spring in the mountains. I was certain that I could often feel Swamiji looking in on me during morning meditation. During the winter I had become a yoga asana fanatic. In what some would see as a very arrogant gesture, I was attempting to revive and revise some obscure yoga kriyas. I was hoping to simplify and remold ancient sets of arcane practices that could promote good health and heighten consciousness. The Source insisted that I dig deep and follow my own intuition and knowing. This infuriated me. Why should I strain so hard and never quite be sure when the answers could easily be given? Intellectually, I understood the task. But emotionally, I was simply revealed as ambivalent and dependent. Although I was eventually satisfied with the kriyas, the real lesson became one of focus, trust, and discernment.

It was now time for spring cleaning, scraping, and painting. We had been in Telluride long enough to see the wet and cold and the hot and dry take its toll on our new home. Putting on some old clothes, I gathered up a wire brush and a metal scraper, then placed the ladder against the side of the house. The sun shone down upon the valley like a great radiant guardian and slowly warmed the hillsides. The entire landscape was turning green. The air was still and intense. The gushing spring runoff was turning the river from a silty mud-laden soup to a clear transparent nectar. It sparkled and shimmered as it rippled under the sun.

Working slowly, working with pleasure, I rubbed my hands across the uneven texture of the rough-sawn cedar siding. The rising sun had made it warm to the touch. As I scraped and brushed the side of the house, a slight scent of fresh cedar filled my nostrils. It was a day full of grace and beauty. It was the kind of day that prompts one to say, "It just doesn't get any better than this." As the sun rose higher in the sky, I began to have longer and longer periods of motionless joy. I found myself filled with solemn appreciation for the gift of being allowed to live within the sacred valley.

While I listened to the intermittent tapping of a carpenter's hammer echoing across the street, I became aware of two crows that were squabbling. They hopped, screeched, and fluttered. They flew over the house and sat upon power poles, craning their necks with great curiosity. They would stand on one leg and then the other. They would puff up their feathers, stretch their wings, and plunge into warm eddies of air that had begun to flow across the canyon. They got closer and closer. One landed on the ground a few yards away and pretended it wasn't the least bit interested in what I was doing. I decided to move toward him. He glared at me and then leapt into the air and belched forth a loud scolding squawk.

It was time for lunch. I went into the house and found my beloved typing away on her word processor. She was involved in a rush job for the court in Tucson. With the modern miracle of overnight express mail and the computerized modem, her court transcribing business had remained intact. The children were somewhere across the river, playing in the park. Stepping out on the deck, she called them to come and eat. We began to prepare turkey and avocado sandwiches that were laced with generous portions of onion and tomatoes. This was a snack that the Source had once suggested as "meeting the essential requirements of the bodies."

Turning toward the mountain, I saw one of the ravens landing on the railing of the deck. It began to watch us through the open door. It glared intently with its head, shoulders, and tail feathers all in one straight horizontal line. I was amazed at how large it looked as we carefully watched each other. Without interrupting its gaze, it rotated its head forty-five degrees, stood up straight, and cawed. It waddled around a moment, then dove back into the air. As I turned to my wife, I could sense that the Source was with her and about to speak. The Source had been on one of its long, unannounced vacations. It hadn't been around for a couple of months. After a few moments came a gently chiding voice from the Source.

"Don't you recognize an invitation when you see one?" Well, I guess I didn't. I had to be told.

This was basically what was said. It was suggested that I watch the birds, follow them and see where they might lead. We sat in silence for a moment, then went on with lunch as the kids stormed into the house. After we had finished, she looked at me with those dark peaceful eyes that had first captured my heart and said, "Well, don't you think you need to get going?" Nodding in agreement, we exchanged hugs. I bounced down the steps, filled my canteen, and proceeded to follow two raving ravens onto the north slope.

After a while, I was feeling sort of foolish. I half ran and half crawled up the hillside under the probable delusion that these black-winged creatures were inviting me to go somewhere. During the chase I passed a couple of recreational hikers who noticed my off-trail route and propensity to watch for glimpses of the circling birds. They sort of wondered out loud what I was doing.

I attempted to make a casual explanation. However, I could tell from the incredulous looks on their faces that they were not accepting of my adventure. It turned out that their main concern was that I must be in violation of some Forest Service mandate because I wasn't staying on the trail. Any attempt to explain further seemed to be pointless, so I shrugged them off and continued my outlaw journey.

Before long, the birds could no longer be found. The last time I saw them, they were headed into a flat wooded area just above what eventually became an obscure extension of Jud Wiebe Trail. Drenched in perspiration and gasping for air, I finally conceded that I had lost sight of the crows. I lay down on the spongy ground and waited for my heart to slow its pounding. I was lying within an old-growth forest that looked like it had once been thinned, probably by some old-timer looking for timber to shore up a tunnel.

The older trees cast deep shadows across grass that was growing in soil still moist from melting snow. Where there had once been a small artificial clearing, there were now dozens of healthy young aspen and evergreens standing eight to fifteen feet tall. Rising out of the darkened forest floor, they were clamoring for whatever light their hungry leaves could capture. Here and there were decaying logs that might have been cut down a hundred years ago. Although near the trail, this was a quiet, secluded place where not many people would venture. As I recovered my breath and surveyed the area, I recognized it as a place that I had visited with friends in my youth.

Within this little basin there had always been a sense of darkness and foreboding. I remembered that one of my schoolmates had claimed that your voice would make an echo if you could find the precise center of this wooded park. We never found it. I was surprised at how, after all these years, the place still felt anguished and haunted. It was cool, sitting in the shade, but it seemed that there was more to the coldness than mere temperature. Everything was incredibly quiet. I was impressed with how the forest was healing itself. A casual observer might not notice that there had ever been any damage.

I once again began to wonder about the crows. They were gone. I had lost them. As I sat in the stillness, I found myself resisting dark heavy feelings that seemed to pull at my body. I finally admitted that I had stumbled back into a place that had always been more than a little intimidating. That feeling had not gone away just because I had grown up.

Waiting to see what I would do next, I noticed that I had begun to meditate. However, the peace that was experienced earlier that morning was nowhere to be found. The meditation was calm and focused, but it was just ordinary. As I climbed to my feet, I placed the palm of my hand against an old aspen in order to steady myself. There began a faint sensation of pulling and clutching, as if the tree had grabbed hold and didn't want to let go of my hand. In my mind's eye I began to see slight flickering of an image, but it was easily passed off as fantasy.

I considered removing my hand from the tree. However, the longer it was there, the more it felt comfortable and inviting. So I allowed it to linger, casually savoring the sensation of the smooth texture of the white, chalky bark. The image began to reappear and became clearer. There was some sort of being standing right where I was standing, placing its hand right where my hand was being placed. A bit startled but still curious, I remained still and attempted to establish communication. It just stood there. It was either ignoring me or just unaware of my inquiring mind. It continued to hold its hand to the tree. I felt like I was being mocked.

The spirit, as I shall call him, had long flowing jet black hair. The body was thin and graceful. It didn't seem threatening, but there was something rather peculiar about it. Then I realized that, although I had assumed it was a male, it didn't really have any gender. It was wrapped in soft white clothing that reminded me of the bark of the aspen. Shaking off the impressions, I sat back down, leaned against a fallen tree, and opened my eyes. Taking a deep breath, I relaxed into the curiosity of my mind and noticed that the being was still there. This time it was sitting down, again right in the same place where I was sitting, resting in the same position. I found myself attempting to listen to its thoughts, but it didn't seem to be having any. It had attention and focus and something that felt like compassion, but it was a compassion devoid of emotionalism. I turned to the right and to the left and still it was there. It stayed right with me. It would not allow me to see its face. It would look where I would look and focus on whatever would be my focus.

Then there were some fleeting nuances of irritation and disbelief as the being realized that I didn't know who "he" was or what to think of him. Recognizing this, the spirit began to radiate a sense of peace and patience. The being was intensely involved with nurturing the earth and plant life. It seemed that it was looking to me to provide some kind of assistance and direction. The being was engaged in mirroring and somehow expanding whatever I would do. It was as if it was lending me its power and could increase the strength and focus of whatever I would decide to do. In this manner, each of us was stronger than we would be if we worked separately. It was inviting me to join with it. As the communing continued, I was being introduced to another realm. All this was done without words, but through feelings, images and a kind of intuitive knowing.

I began to wonder what it was about this place that made it feel so haunted. The spirit, responding to my thoughts, looked into the darkened forest and out came a being wearing a headdress of some kind of horned animal. He raised a primitive spear and shook it at me as if he were chastising and warning me to stay away. The dark-haired spirit felt my uneasiness and became slightly protective and calming, as if to say, don't worry about him, he doesn't like anyone, he always acts that way. Then he turned another direction and I briefly saw what looked like a face that was made out of bark. However, it didn't seem to know that anyone else was there or was watching. Its consciousness seemed dull and a little perplexed. It turned its head for a moment, then looked back with a startled response. When it looked in my direction the second time, it seemed to be seeing me for the first time. After a moment, it retreated into a darkened place within an old rotting stump.

I rested a moment, attempting to sort out my impressions. I found myself floundering, impatient to know more. What were these things that I was encountering? What were their intentions and what were they wanting from me? I sensed the spirit of the aspen one more time. It grew long and narrow, like a river flowing or a cloud stretching into a lofty current of wind. It left me and placed a long graceful hand back on the tree. I could sense dozens of entities with different levels of understanding and intention, all watching, some in fear, some angry or intimidated. My thought was suspended as I stretched deeply into a new world of sensation. I questioned and wondered what my inner eyes were seeing.

Then I realized what I had been witnessing. These were what some teachings call the dakini, the spirits and elementals that live just beyond our perception in the astral and ethereal realms. They often hover close to the earth, just beyond our perceptions, bridging the gap between the material and the spiritual realms. They come in many sizes, forms, and shapes. They are not necessarily good or evil, but over time they can become influenced, molded, and stained by encounters with human beings. They have many origins and purposes. Some are related to the basic elements and the four directions. There are supposedly legions of them involved with the process of keeping the planet fertile and helping plants and animals grow.

I had come with the hope of finding some answers to my spiritual questing. Hoping for something to show me what I should be doing about this enchanted mountain that had called to me and altered my life course. A faint impression began to form that continued to grow in intensity and clarity. It seemed I was being invited to this place to serve as some sort of catalyst or fulcrum. I had been brought to this strange place to engage in some kind of dialogue and healing in order to re-establish harmony and order.

The spirits and elementals of this place were reeling in disarray. Many of these had come into being during the earliest times of the original exploration, when human souls reached through and into the dense material plane. Passing through the sensitive ethereal membranes and veils, many helpers and adversaries had been both attracted and created. This was during the eons in which we were slowly becoming enmeshed in the earth, stretching deeper and deeper into the rock, plants, and flesh of this material realm.

As ignorance and greed began to well up from descending human souls, there ensued a vicious battle in which some of the elemental forces had been captured, harnessed, and twisted for selfish and perverse ends. These dueling sorcerers, drawing upon the primal forces of the earth, eventually passed into an oblivion of their own creation. They moved onward into the encrusted and hardened consciousness that began to limit their mischievous conduct. They were no longer able to practice their profane occupations in the quest for power and domination within the ethereal realms.

These battles now rage between sorcerers in other arenas. However, their ways have become crude and less sophisticated. A few of these ancient sorcerers have returned and now walk within the ranks of those that call themselves scientists. Their battles are raging on within the modern technocratic confines of particle dispersion physics and genetic engineering.

There is a way of working with the natural order and a way of usurping it for selfish domination. The inhabitants of a sleeping planet await the outcome of their continued tampering. In general, they tend to mock the natural order of things. They are adding greatly to the anguish of the planet, but some are learning and are slowly recovering from their maddening blindness.

The primary purpose of these particular dakini is to be as the guardians of the earth, to keep the pure spirit and power of creation alive and resplendent. Many of them also stand ready to point the way for pilgrims who periodically come to remember the source and purpose of their sojourn into the planet.

In the wake of the sorcerers' descent into the earth, there were left patches of sacred ground such as this one, turned into turmoil through corruption and trickery. Many of the spirit beings that huddled together within this little grove remained angry, resentful, and suspicious. While some waited patiently, struggling to promote healing and forgiveness, others continued to hang onto their guilt, shame, and rage. These debilitating energies are often used as a shield or a weapon against the psychic and physical pain that was anciently inflicted upon them by their perpetrators who eventually became human.

In a later time, the people had recognized this place and began to use it as a place of questing, remembering, and teaching. It became a place of sacred ceremony and demonstrated the capacity for renewal and rejoicing. A great healing was taking place.

Hearts were glad, and the people danced. However, in the midst of their celebration they were cut down by another roving group of people who knew little of healing ways. These intruders had become heavily invested in the enemy way. Once again, the land soaked up the energies of betrayed and anguished souls. The ancient terror was revived and began to radiate through the ground and into the bedrock that had absorbed the recurrent folly. This was a primal garden that had been abandoned by the ancient ones as they continued their plunge into forgetfulness.

During a more recent encounter, a new kind of human had come. He was blind, unable to see or to feel the presence of the spirit beings. He was ignorant of the ways of the natural world, unable to understand the nature of either tortured or sacred ground. He had no greeting, did not ask permission, and left no offering for the lumber he was harvesting. This man began to feel discomfort, but he had no understanding of its nature or its source. He became more and more uncomfortable. He may have had nightmares. He eventually took his crew and left the area and never returned. In his wake lay fallen trees and churned ground. Those activities had once again revived the ancient terror that still permeated the area.

I realized that within this little grove there still abides an ancient guardian who helps the aspen grow. The spirit of the aspen continues healing, trusting and waiting for the people to remember and to return to a circle of harmony and balance.

I cannot say if these spirits and memories that blossomed within my mind's eye were real. Perhaps they were merely symbolic representations, presented in ways for the conscious mind to be able to grasp and understand. After a while, I could no longer see or feel the one that I have come to call the guardian spirit of the aspen. I sat humbled and troubled. My mind fought the images and experiences that I had just seen, felt, and heard. It resisted. It rebutted. It challenged, chastised, and questioned its sanity. It tried to call the vision an absurd fantasy. However, it seemed the mind was protesting too much. I went with my feelings and listened to my heart. Anguish began to rise to my throat. First came a moaning, then a chanting as I began to sing. Standing between two trees, I stretched my arms outward and placed my hands upon them and continued my unintelligible song. I was calling for blessing, for healing, seeking compassion for all that had been wronged. At one point I could swear I could hear aspen acknowledging my presence and singing along.

Soon emotion was spent and it was time to go. Moving through the small, wooded basin, I looked down beside the path and happened to see the skeleton of some animal. It was too large to be a sheep. I thought it might be a calf, but it was probably a deer or an elk. It was old, partially buried in the ground. Many of the bones were scattered. The remaining bones were bleached, brittle, and cracked. Rummaging through the grass, I discovered a badly fractured skull. It had been an antlered animal. I picked it up and placed it on the ground at the top of the remaining spinal column. I think I sprinkled some loose dirt across it as I said a brief prayer.

Continuing down into the valley, I noticed a single cloud in an otherwise cloudless sky. It had formed over the sacred grove, within the forest, next to the trail. Before long the cloud thinned out in the center and formed a circular shape that hovered for a few moments. Then it broke apart and drifted down toward the valley as it disappeared.

That night I had a dream. The threatening figure that I had seen that day was standing over the skeleton. It wore a mask that completely covered the head. At first it looked like a buffalo, then a deer or an elk. It nodded a greeting of approval and thumped the butt of a primitive spear into the ground four times. It turned, drifted into a light that radiated from somewhere deep within the forest, and melted away.

The Source claimed that this was part of the reason I had been summoned back to the mountain. It expressed the hope that I would continue to have these kinds of experiences; this is all a part of the path. I pressed for more explanations and conclusions. There was an admonishment not to always try to understand everything. It was explained that sometimes it is best to just experience an event and to allow your understanding to unfurl as it will.

I was gently chastised and told that I already knew this and should stop fishing for external explanations. I was also reminded that there are obligations for anyone who seeks to follow a spiritual path. I was supposedly brought to the mountain for remembering and for teachings. For there to be true spiritual growth, there needs to be ever-growing compassion and healing. And it was acknowledged that each of us must learn how to become an active part of that healing process.

In the months and years that followed, the secluded grove became a place that I would visit often. It became a place of pilgrimage, and eventually a place where others would be invited for their own initiations. As I share my heart and ceremonies within this sacred place, it slowly becomes less anguished, more peaceful. With proper intent, each visit releases a little more of the turmoil and induces healing in all who would participate.

Chapter Nine

The Conquest of Paradise

For some reason, people tend to believe that they are the first ones of any consequence to come on the scene. What has gone on before is usually discounted and misunderstood, if not altogether ignored. Through the generations we forget much of our history.

Just north of Cortez, Colorado we once visited a museum exhibit that featured some translations of a Jesuit journal describing an expedition, which included the Telluride region. This expedition took place in the early 1600s. When these pilgrims arrived, it was noticed that they discovered some crude wood and leather Spanish-style rockers, which were used in an attempt to do some placer mining. It was obvious that gold-seeking conquistadors had been there before the arrival of the Jesuit who made the entries in the journal. Later, when they were stranded in slide rock, a Ute Indian showed them a high mountain pass that led them safely through what eventually became known as the Telluride Valley.

In the Telluride Medical Clinic during the late eighties, there was a picture that hung next to the door. It might still be there. As I recall, it looked like a black and white lithograph of some kind. With a typical San Juan Mountain backdrop, there stood a man dressed in buckskin and a fur cap and holding some kind of musket. I believe he had a bit of a beard. The man's name was James Gardiner. Underneath was a caption heralding him as one of the first explorers into the Telluride Valley. This supposedly occurred sometime just before the gold rush of the 1870s. There seems to be the assumption that nothing was here before the surveyors came. I've always found the picture to be a bit revealing. It exemplifies not only the way we tend to conduct journalism, but the way most generations write history.

As the exploration and trapping era came to an end, the Native American Indians were rather ungraciously moved out in order to make the region safe for the new and inevitable modern era. Although there were a few scattered ranching homesteads upon the mesas and along the rivers, the main interest of the new horde was the quest for gold and silver. Soon, thousands of hopeful prospectors invaded the high country in search of riches. After a few years there was a massive consolidation. A few large mining companies, with their ability to attract large capital investment and to operate more efficiently, eventually took over much of the local mining industry. Most of the surviving companies slowly merged into one major company that was internationally owned. Then, for several decades, Telluride became a quiet, shrinking one-company town, dependent upon the fluctuating price of the minerals that were harvested from the mountains.

Out of the 1960s came another invasion. The town became overrun by a new breed in search of their generation's vision of paradise. For a while this invasion of thought, dress, and lifestyle created a bit of a battle for control of the community's political structure. It was the old-timers against the hippies. Some of the fighting was comical, and some was pathetically tragic. I sincerely believe that some people never noticed that anything was changing until it was too late to seriously consider other alternatives.

In the seventies, as the mine closed, the seductive lure of an economy based on skiing and land speculation gripped the community. By the early eighties, construction and real estate became the economy. Skiing was only a sideline that lured people into the valley to speculate in real estate. Skiing doesn't tend to make money, but it usually brings a new wave of conquistadors who continue the tradition of trampling over the previous generations' version of paradise.

Thus, the seeds of modern progress began to take hold. The vision of the sacred valley of the sixties and seventies became a negative ideology, which impaired the potential to become a world class resort. Most of the "hippies" who were not trustfunders, either left town or became Builder Realtors and developers. In town, a "too little too late" attempt was made to salvage a unique but rapidly dying lifestyle. Meanwhile, a whole resort city was beginning to take shape upon an adjoining mesa.

Once the ski company sponsored contests to see who could grow the best beard; now beards would not be tolerated. There was concern it would frighten the condo-buying yuppies. Yuppies bought real estate, which fed the attorneys, developers, real estate offices, construction crews, and the struggling shops and restaurants that lined Main Street.

Soon, the yuppies would not be able to afford much real estate. Next, the wealthy would be groomed. These are the kind of people who buy condos and houses like most of us rent motel rooms. Most of those who supported the growth in order to get a regular paycheck soon found they couldn't afford to buy a home. Meanwhile, rents skyrocketed. At one point, I noticed that almost seventy percent of the homes in town were owned by people from out of state. The locals lived miles away.

In less than seven years, lots went from $40,000 to $50,000 to $150,000 to $200,000. Houses appreciated from $100,000 to $150,000 to as high as $600,000 to $800,000. Now a modest million-dollar home in the Telluride region is a real bargain, if you can find one. A short drive down valley, speculators could purchase large tracts of ranch land for a few hundred dollars an acre, and within a few years sell forty-acre parcels for $300,000 to $500,000. And the pattern continues.

Many of the local real estate brokers found themselves losing control of the market as seasoned professional developers entered the scene with more sophisticated approaches and almost unlimited access to development capital. The survivors tended to become partners or managers for these foreign interests.

At times, the market is dead; and the computerized listing books swell. At times, there is a stampede as cash-rich entrepreneurs come to grab their slice of paradise. There is as much money lost as made. The market can be volatile. Large mortgages and unfavorable interest rates combined with a little slump can wreak havoc on those caught up in the cyclic buying frenzies. Sometimes people buy what they can't afford during the excitement of the moment. When the market dips, speculators who lack deep pockets and are unable to weather the downturns tend to get caught up in the occasional rash of foreclosures. Disgruntled amateur investors hoping for a quick killing move on in a quest for more attractive investments. However, as any well-capitalized entrepreneur knows, these situations also create the opportunities to amass fortunes in a very short period of time.

One fall, after the construction of the airport, things went particularly crazy. I once took a client out to inspect four separate lots. Upon returning to the office, I discovered that there were already contracts on three of the offerings. One lot already had a "backup" contract, just in case the existing deal fell through. While visiting another brokerage, I heard a gentleman complaining about sales ethics. He wanted to know, "How dumb do you think I am; every other property they show me they claim just sold." He was convinced people were lying to him and trying to trick him. No one wanted to work with him. No one had the time. This was a month when buyers had to make reservations and wait in line to be shown property at Telluride Mountain Village. There weren't enough brokers to show the available listings.

This was a different kind of gold rush. However, the effect on the locals was similar to what the previous land grab had done to the Indians a century before. Once again, the locals would either assimilate into the impending dominant culture, move on, or perish. The new culture brought with it some very strange people with very odd attitudes and values. Too often, they take positions such as: The more a person spends on something, the more valuable the person becomes; you should be pleased that I have come here to show you how you should live and; don't you have any idea of how important I am.

One day a man came into the office and complained that compared to other major ski resorts, Telluride had nothing to offer. He didn't understand the ridiculous prices. We didn't have sufficient services or professional entertainment; many of the streets were gravel; businesses would close during the off season; there weren't enough celebrities in the area, and on and on.

After listening to this for about half an hour, I literally took the gentleman by the arm and led him outside. I insisted he look to the east, the south, the west, and the north and pause a moment after looking in each direction. Then I told him with complete sincerity that, if he didn't find anything he liked, he should leave. I explained that the only thing here of value was the wilderness; the mountains, the waterfalls, the river. If all that he was seeking was the convenience and amusements of modern civilization, then perhaps he should go somewhere else.

I explained that the real thing that made this valley valuable was its beauty and enchantment. I explained that every time another building went up, some of that natural beauty was badly marred. This was a very special place. It is a place that is sacred. I presented the attitude that, if he were blessed enough to have the opportunity to spend some time here he should look deep within himself and identify the reasons he needed to acquire real estate. He was admonished to purchase prudently and unselfishly, in a way that would be for the long-term good of the community and the pristine mountains that surrounded the valley.

He looked startled, shocked, and angry that I would speak to him in such a manner. I wasn't playing the game. I was supposed to tell him whatever fabrications he wanted to hear. I was supposed to tell him of the good deals that I could find for him. I was supposed to tell him about all the money he would make, and how pleased I was to welcome him into my community. Of course, I was to do this in such a way that I couldn't be blamed if his particular investment didn't work out. I was to become his obedient servant, laugh at his vulgar insensitive jokes, make his travel arrangements, pick him up at the airport, introduce him to influential locals, maybe find him a good drug connection, and tell him what great friends we had become.

To my surprise, I soon discovered large tears welling up in his eyes. We went back into the office. He quietly sobbed for a moment; then he talked for over two hours, pouring out his soul, telling me about his life, his divorce, his betrayal by his best friend and business partner. He was coming to the mountain to have his ego soothed. Instead, I had inadvertently lanced his boil. But he really didn't get it. He probably thought the same of me.

As the man left, he invited me for an evening of drunkenness at a local saloon. Not being one to participate in the ritual of recreational drug use, I declined. It was explained that I could be available tomorrow if he wished to talk more. This was a time when sales were very slow. In a place overrun with real estate agents, this was a grievous error.

He bought his trophy house from a Realtor that he met in the bar. It became one of those houses where no one lives except for maybe two to three weeks out of the year when the owner returns to do maintenance. I wasn't very good at being a Realtor or a "dirt pimp," as some people called us. My heart wasn't in it. However, it brought in a little cash and afforded enough free time to continue the various pilgrimages that the Source was constantly suggesting.

The town was becoming a very convoluted place, full of stark contradictions and once-in-a-lifetime opportunities. Festivals were multiplying like rabbits. Hollywood had arrived with all its wealth, splendor and seduction. Streets hummed with rumors of the presence of the rich and famous. You might find Arnold Schwarzenegger visiting our school, or Donald Trump making a purchase at the Telluride Market. Maybe Oprah Winfrey was in town hiking with her trainer or asking my daughter to do some personal Christmas shopping to provide gifts for her entourage. Perhaps Stallone was in town buying a few more lots. Sometimes a governor would show up for a few days. Perhaps you would see Clint Eastwood strolling down Main Street. Some of these people are wonderfully creative, sensitive human beings. Some of them are evil incarnate. Once during the film festival, a wild-eyed young fan grabbed me by the arm and shoved an autograph book and pen in my hand and almost pinned me to the wall. She demanded my signature and then asked me if I was anybody special. I told her yes.

While professors and potheads scurried over the foothills looking for favorite varieties of mushrooms, Rastafarians could be heard beating drums and playing music in the streets. During the yearly cycle of festivals, there was an opportunity to hear just about any kind of music imaginable: bluegrass, jazz, rock, classical, or maybe the simple melody of a homemade flute.

Physicists of the world would congregate to debate the course of particle dispersion theory and plot their next generation of experiments. Perhaps a national politician or TV evangelist would park his plane at the airport for a weekend. A festival for new age groupies, airheads, and other budding pagans blossomed as sweat lodges were built in the town park and talking circles were conducted on a community soccer field. So-called fringe groups massed to bring attention to issues of deforestation and global warming. The Source said we should be more concerned about a possible ice age.

As all this was going on, an occasional black bear might wander into town. In the morning you could sometimes locate a few bewildered elk or deer standing in the shadows up in the foothills. If it was fall, they might get killed, and controversy would rage. Watching from the deck of my home, you could marvel at avalanches in the winter and fireworks in July.

One day, Art Goodtimes, a local journalist and politician, handed me the talking gourd at the poetry festival; and poetry became my passion. All this in a place where the family dog could bark at hot air balloons in the spring and hang gliders in the fall, floating just a hundred feet over our home.

At the real estate office, I chatted with investors from Switzerland and Colombia. Sometimes a retired diplomat would wander in looking for the best place in town to eat or an opportunity to use a copier or fax machine. Once, a self-styled Ute medicine man cornered me on the street claiming this was Indian land. He kept challenging me to a battle of sorcery. I had a long, bizarre conversation followed by a very vivid dream in which the man attempted to stuff my soul into an old leather medicine bag. The next two times I saw this Indian he would become very agitated, start muttering to himself, and walk away. He eventually left town, drunk. The Source claimed our dream battle was real, and lamented that the man's energies were so woefully misdirected.

During the mega-festivals, you might find a stranger using your shower or relieving himself (or herself) in your front yard. One day while my children played in front of the house, two anxious-looking men approached me rather forcefully, insisting that I sell them some drugs. Nothing I said seemed to convince them that I didn't do that sort of thing. But, after all, I lived in Telluride, had long hair, and wore a beard; and they knew what Telluride was all about.

I finally did admit that I knew someone who had experience in these matters. I gave them a phone number and asked them not to give it out to anyone else. I suggested that these people would know how to take care of them. In a few moments they came running back to their car and sped westward down Main Street and out of town. The number I had given them was the San Miguel County Sheriff's dispatch number. I don't think they appreciated my peculiar sense of humor.

In a local pizza pub there was a picture displayed from the Ophir side of the "Blixt-Hunter Highway." It had deteriorated to a trail suitable for mountain bikes and hiking. It was intended to be a haulage road linking the upper basin to the Ophir valley. My father had built it in the late fifties when he and Oscar were mining partners in the high country. A photographer was offering this photograph for sale, calling it the "Blitzed Highway." When I questioned the name and who had built it, the waiter assured me that I must be mistaken because the artist was a local and everything he did was authentic. Who was I to question an authentic local?

One year the park was made available for winter camping in order to help maintain the town's unskilled labor force. From my window I could sometimes see people huddled around fires in deep snow while most of the homes in my neighborhood sat vacant. I don't believe that I'm a capitalist or a socialist. I'm something else. I realize that many of those people in that park were not interested in working very hard. And the owners of the houses were often sacrificing themselves to earn money doing things they despised so that they could occasionally visit their investments and dream of opulent retirement in the midst of pristine wilderness that is rapidly deteriorating. However, the sheer paradox of the situation was a bit too bizarre for me to comprehend.

One day, while walking up Bear Creek Canyon, I discovered several people living in homeless shelters propped up against some shallow caves created by some overhanging outcroppings. Earlier that day, I was witness to a couple fighting over whether or not they wanted to fly to Norway to bid on a yacht they had been hoping to acquire. I found the diversity invigorating, exciting, and comical. Where else but in Telluride could such opposing lifestyles, economies, and ideologies collide with such gusto and grace.

The town of Telluride was rapidly being swallowed up. The valley floor was shrinking. It was beginning to look like Disneyland, San Francisco, MTV, and a county fair all rolled into one huge construction project. Some of the changes were welcome and fascinating. Some of the changes were revolting. But what the town would become was of no consequence. In my mind, I was there for the duration, hanging on with both hands, at the request of something that lunged up from the depth of my being.

Good or bad, none of these helter-skelter activities in the valley made any difference. I wasn't there for the town. I had returned to commune with the mountain.

Chapter Ten

Jaguar Kiva

The Source claimed there were natural kivas, or topographical centers, within the earth that are full of the power and spirit of ancient teachings and traditions. Some of these are associated with certain kachinas and animal clans. It seems that, according to this information, kachinas are similar to angels in that they originally came into existence in order to exemplify certain aspects of the godhead. They tend to provide a particular spiritual focus that can be used to assist and guide human beings. They sometimes appear during periods of great need or transition. These creations became necessary because, after the separation from the oneness and our descent into the material plane, direct communication with the Creator had become more and more difficult. These spirit beings can take many different forms, depending upon the needs of the times and the cultural influences into which they come. They often assist us without our conscious understanding or awareness. Many have existed since our earliest embodiment into the earth. These particular teachings were of special interest to me because there was this one such location that tended to capture my attention and imagination ever since I was a child. According to the Source, this was a place of emergence for one of the animal clan kachinas.

As a young boy, I recalled bouncing along in Dad's pink Jeep and gazing up into this huge oval shaped ravine. It seemed both inviting and mysterious. I had fantasized that someday I might even build a cabin on that site. In some places the high red cliffs were almost orange and purple. The ravine sported a small intermittent stream that was active during the spring thaw and sometimes lasted into the early summer.

One day I found myself feeling very restless. Something was stirring. The town was feeling too cramped, too crowded. So I decided it was time to visit this place that had called to me for over thirty years. Winchester, the family dog, was used to my excursions into wilderness. Cued by my preparations, he seemed to know it was time for a hike. Being unable to resist the enthusiasm of his wagging tail, I decided to take my loyal companion along. Parking next to the highway, I grabbed my small blue backpack and climbed over the barbed-wire fence. I was trespassing, but I didn't think anyone would mind. This was part of one of the old ranches that was being subdivided. As a Realtor it was important to know your product, so I figured there was adequate reason to investigate the area without formal permission. After all, like everything else, it was for sale.

There was not any particular goal or expectation. I just wanted to go there, spend some time, meditate, and enjoy the solitude. The summer grass was beginning to turn brown due to the lack of rain. Moisture from the winter snows had long ago evaporated from the hard-cracked soil. There was a bit of a game trail, but there were no fresh tracks. While walking the several hundred yards toward this natural earth kiva, I stumbled over a loose rock and found myself wincing as I twisted an ankle. After entering the sanctuary, I sat down and rested my throbbing tendons. Winchester and I had stopped within a little clearing surrounded by evergreen trees. It was perhaps twenty or thirty feet across and located in the heart of the ravine.

I was feeling tight and irritable. My mind raced with thoughts of real estate and finances. The hope of one pointed consciousness was far away. Deer flies buzzed around my face, biting at the droplets of perspiration on my forehead. After discovering that I was sitting on an ant hill, I moved from the center of the clearing and rested in the shade of a clump of young pine trees.

I watched the dog race around the sage and oak brush. He loved to be let loose. In town he had become a prisoner. Although he would periodically escape, his life was limited to the house or the end of a leash or chain. It was good to watch him run, sniff, and roll in the dirt. I shared in the excitement of his moments of glorious freedom.

I was beginning to feel a little more peaceful. However, my mind was still charging around with all the turmoil of a frightened squirrel, just like the one that was being chased by Winchester. Fortunately, the critter had sense enough to run up a tree. After some friendly "rough-housing" with my coyote brother, I limped over to one of the pine trees, pulled a folding knife out of my pocket and extended the blade. This was the last gift my father had given me before he died. My thumb ran gently over the sharpened edge, just the way he had always told me not to do, just the way he had always done.

With a free hand upon a tree, I said a quiet prayer, asking for permission to commune with this special place. Next, eight pine boughs were cut. Each one was about six to eight inches in length. I was particularly drawn to boughs that contained three budding branches. Eight branches of sage were also cut. Returning to the edge of the clearing, I placed the boughs and branches around me, alternating the sage and pine. Clearing away some of the grass and pine needles, I lit a stick of incense and stuck it into the sandy earth. Around the incense I placed a few sprigs of blossoming yarrow. There wasn't a particular plan. Each step just seemed like the proper thing to do. Sitting quietly, I savored the rich fragrances of the fresh cut pine and sage that mixed with the yarrow and incense. The air was still. The smoky plume of incense rose straight up for several inches before swirling into an ever-expanding vortex that slowly dissipated.

I took off my boots and socks and poured some water from my canteen onto my feet and carefully massaged the aching ankle. Then I took a long slow swig, savoring the simple pleasure of the cool refreshing water that quenched the thirst of my parched throat. Raising the canteen over my head, a few ounces of the precious liquid dribbled through my hair into my scalp and down through my beard. I rubbed the excess across my face and around the back of my neck with the palms of my hands. It was good to feel the evaporating water cooling the skin and relaxing the muscles.

Noticing a panting little tongue, I shared some of this refreshing natural brew with my furry, four-footed friend. Sitting cross legged in the circle, I began to chant. After some howling and barking, Winchester lay down next to me and fell asleep. Eventually, I unstrapped the handmade drum that hung from my backpack and placed it on the ground before me. It had been purchased at Taos Pueblo the previous winter during one of the Source's pilgrimages.

Feeling a little self-conscious and awkward, I thumped at the drum a few times and chuckled out loud as I asked myself, "Would you buy real estate from this man?" The impromptu ceremony continued; a timid uneven beat began to fill the secluded little canyon. Closing my eyes, listening to the growing rhythm, I soon became aware that the pounding of the drum and the beating of my heart had become synchronized. I don't know how long the drumming lasted. It may have been an hour or more. Emotion began to rise up within me. I beat out my hopes, my anger, my frustration, and my shame, sometimes pounding wildly and rapidly, sometimes thumping the smooth surface gently and lovingly. Tears from an unknown well filled my eyes and dripped onto this throbbing altar of pagan compassion.

Time seemed to disappear. Inside my physical body there eventually emerged the sensation of an inner soul body, twisting, shaking, swirling, and tumbling. Staring into a vast shadowy cavern, I began to feel the warmth of moist breath. Out of incredulous silence, a quiet ripple of intermittent murmuring began to caress my straining ears. From out of an abyss of incredible darkness, two almost invisible specks of golden light appeared. They began to move closer becoming larger, glowing brighter. Before long I discovered I was staring deeply into a pair of piercing eyes. They were powerful, fierce, and challenging. They seemed to be evaluating me for some unknown purpose. I wondered if this were some satanic demon and began to feel a little panicked; I wanted to look away. Somehow I knew I should just trust, stay calm, and keep looking.

Suddenly, I could feel myself running, jumping, lunging across the landscape, flowing like water over sculpted rock, claws stretching, clutching and releasing, effortlessly gliding across rich red earth. I was alive. I was wild, scampering in silence through canyons, grasslands and forests; huddling motionlessly at the meadow's edge; watching, waiting, searching from quiet, restful shadows with a purpose and patience that could outlive hardened granite. My heart was beating with the fierceness of the darkened jaguar, cousin of the cougar. It was a heart of unbridled freedom, a heart of savage passion, and a heart of quiet wisdom. I became one with its relentless power, compassionate intention, and intense manner.

Peering through the shadows, there came an offering of sacred knowledge, a conscious vision, a dreaming while awake. From out of the glowing darkness came prayer feathers to be used for sacred pilgrimage, an altar for discovering and remembering one's path upon the earth, and a rattle for listening and focusing on that which would always lead one safely back home. Then he revealed himself. There in the silence stood an ancient being who had long ago been forgotten, yet continuing its vigil as a guardian of an ancient and sacred way.

With a swirling of gold, crimson, and violet there came a flash of brilliant light that filled me with waves of penetrating heat that reluctantly faded. Opening my eyes and stretching out my legs, I laid back on the ground wondering about what had just happened. It was more than a fantasy, more than a dream. It was another vivid dream that had happened while I was still awake. The presence of this sacred beast lingered. It seemed there was an after-image of still, fierce eyes offering wisdom that reached out from an ancient and primal place. Standing and stretching, I began to breathe deeply. Quickly, the images and feelings began to fade. My senses began to stabilize and return to their normal state. I picked up my gear and headed back down the trail. It was getting late. Time for dinner. Time to get home.

Taking one last look around the landscape, I began to wonder if these experiences were real. I watched my mind shift from a place of complete confidence and knowing to a place of doubt and questioning. I wondered if I was just whipping up frantic emotions that were being released in these vivid hallucinatory experiences. Perhaps I was falling victim to the power of suggestion from all the pilgrimages and my fascination with Native American Indian practices.

I was looking downward, walking the trail carefully, having no desire to further injure my weakened ankle. I began to wonder about the point of all this. Even if these experiences were real and the teachings were true, what difference would it make in the real world where we all live?

After cautiously navigating a rocky portion of the path, I looked up to see my faithful companion, Winchester. He was riveted, every muscle frozen. I looked to where he was looking. I saw a huge black cat with slightly darker, almost invisible stripes. It was strolling along less than fifty feet away. It was smooth, graceful, and powerful. Its long, black tail trailed downward almost to the ground, then curled upward. It gently swayed from side to side with each silent step. It turned its head. As I saw the eyes, I knew it was the jaguar of my vision. But this time my eyes were open, and the dog saw it too. Winchester was terrified. He began to tremble and started glancing at me with an hysterical whimper as if he were begging for protection.

After a few more steps, the phantom cat faded and disappeared. The panicked dog looked in my direction, then searched where the cat had been. He howled and barked and ran back and forth across the trail, sniffing and panting. The only tracks I could find were mine, Winchester's, and some decaying deer prints. Overcome by primal emotion, tears of relief and gratitude flowed freely down my face as a strange combination of torment and joy was released. It was as if there had begun a cleansing that gushed up from the depths of the soul.

We continued down the path. The mind was still. The presence had been strong. When we got to the Jeep, the dog frantically lunged into the vehicle. Once again something magical had happened upon the mountain. I shook off the visionary cloak and pulled onto the highway. Winchester placed his head in my lap and watched me very carefully all the way home. Once again, it was time to return to the common reality of a modern world.

*   *   *   *   *

Festival season was in full swing. During the coming months there would be a continuous litany of banners across Main Street heralding the next contingent of high country groupies. Throughout the summer and into the fall, each wave would be enticed to the mountain by a conference or activity centered on one of their favorite pastimes. As in previous seasons, they would parade through the town like casually drifting schools of fish, being constantly eyed by the hopeful anglers of the hungry businesses that line Colorado Avenue. Eating and drinking establishments, T-shirt shops, and real estate offices seem to do best. The new age, poetry, whitewater, wine, and balloon festivals were already over. However, the music festivals had not even begun. It has almost become a tradition that each year another event is added to the fare. This year would be no different. Another fledgling conference was being spawned. This year a forum for Native American writers was emerging from the Telluride cradle. This year the Indians were coming! My curiosity was at its peak. Here would be an opportunity to see and meet some of the Native American Indians that write the books, tell the stories, and strive to keep their pagan cultures alive. It would be an opportunity to make contact with those who "talk the talk and walk the walk." It would be a chance to mingle with the recognized and informed. The primary focus of the workshop would be dialogue between the writers. But there were also public sessions. All would be welcome.

*   *   *   *   *

I took a center seat in the Sheridan Opera House. It had just been restored to the image of what its most recent owners believed it should have been. It was a relief that the building wasn't packed. The number of people in the audience wasn't much bigger than the number of participants on the panel. They were supporting and affirming each other rather than catering to the needs or expectations of a white audience. This was great. This was the way it should be.

Eventually, the dialogue began to erupt with some allegations that resulted in some rather offensive philosophical positions. During a brief interchange regarding the environment, there was a demand to know what kind of leadership and direction Native American Indians could provide. After all, they often see themselves as the guardians of the land. The Native American panel generally made it clear that their cultures had not contributed to the environmental problems of the planet. It was up to the dominant culture to take responsibility and to decide what it would do about the problems it had created.

As the session progressed, it became obvious that there was a growing and well-deserved resentment regarding the "new age airheads" gushing over the "vibrations" of things sacred, acting as if they knew all about Native Americans, when all too often they were just responding to the trendy fads in fashion, art, and decor. It was suggested that many of them did not really understand and had never experienced anything sacred in their lives. There was an attitude that sacredness is a thing that only Indians can fully comprehend. It was also expressed that whites are unable to grasp the essence of bonding with a clan or group and can't relate to the sense of unity and belonging that binds together the Indian cultures.

Although there was a lot of healthy ventilation, the discussions also brought out a kind of division and defensiveness that tended to permeate the rest of the conference. Even though the arguments were often articulate and insightful, they tended to be full of muffled rage and anger. And sometimes it wasn't all that muffled.

The anguish and resentment born of a long history of brutal genocide, exploitation, and suppression was intermittently spewing forth. It was a righteous anger, full of dignity and decorum, but spewing just the same. There was a sense that this was their conference, and the ignorance and bigotry of the whites would not be tolerated. However, some of them were oblivious to their own ignorance and bigotry.

Nevertheless, I sought out the counsel of those who I believed should know. I privately asked if they could direct me to anyone who had knowledge of the sacred sites within the San Juan Mountains. I asked individually if they knew of anyone who might have information regarding the ancient animal clans born throughout the Telluride Region. I inquired as to whether or not there was anyone who knew of existing ceremonies or rituals performed to honor these sacred and shining mountains. During the impromptu breaks, I privately shared a little of the jaguar vision and explained that I needed to speak with people who had knowledge and understandings of such things. I wondered out loud if there might be someone I could contact who might help me to understand the essence of my vision. I hoped there was someone who could help put the vision in the jaguar kiva into some kind of fruitful perspective.

There was an attempt to make contact with a lady from a Southwestern nation who is known for her poetry. She reeled back with great suspicion and shock on her face. I began to realize that she was so conditioned by the evil that she saw lurking within blue eyes that she was unable to see me objectively and hear what I was saying. Although confident and articulate when at the podium, she seemed confused and frightened of the implications of the questions that were being presented to her. Looking back at the circumstances, she may have felt I was simply mocking her heritage.

One Indian gentleman who rose to notoriety through scholarship within the university setting purposefully ignored me as he talked to over fifteen Native Americans before he would consider even acknowledging my presence. As he mused at how he made me wait, he finally consented to speak with me when everyone else had gone. He heard little of what I had to say and interrupted frequently and abruptly. He stated over and over again that I might feel the land was special, but the only way for a white person to understand is to talk to the local Indians that know the area. He intimated that it was not really possible for a white person to have an authentic vision on Indian land. He seemed totally unable or unwilling to share with me his experience with me or to consider a time and place where we might speak further.

A white-looking Indian from a large eastern metropolitan area kept muttering that white people just didn't understand what was going on here. A white observer quietly questioned if it might be better if the meeting should be a private conclave and asked if non-Indians should leave. Looking even more perturbed, the urban warrior decided it would be all right with him if the white audience wished to stay as long as they didn't interrupt anything. After that point, I noticed that some of the more stoic and perhaps wiser participants began to avoid public comment or personal contact.

One night there was a banquet for all the participants in the event. In attendance was a wild and passionate young woman. She was full of poetry, the suffering of the earth and the desire to live a full and righteous life. She had just returned from Poland where she had made her own personal pilgrimage. Like many others, she had come to spend some time with the mountain. She would work where she could and usually camped near the river. She was turned away from the banquet by dismayed Indians who could not believe that a white person could have no home or be hungry. These were Indians who could not believe that anyone who lived in Telluride might be hungry and out of money.

Later on, it was hoped that there might be some drumming. It was asked if the Indians would join with us or show us how to do drumming in a sacred manner. However, there was no response, no interest. There were excuses about how the time wasn't right or the drums offered were in too poor condition or not authentic. They looked awkward, embarrassed, and offended.

I slowly began to realize that many of the participants at the gathering had gained their success and notoriety by being absorbed into the dominant culture's methods of marketing. Sometimes there is a fine line between successful marketing and exploitation. Some of the writers live in large cities or have a very limited Indian heritage. They use the same system of universities, publishers, books and conferences from the same system that they were tending to criticize. Some were working to help Indian political causes. Some were working to preserve cultural traditions, legends and history. But in order to be personally successful and keep their causes alive, it would be necessary to continue to sell their books to the dominant (white) American culture.

It should be noted that some of the participants were gifted storytellers who simply shared their writings, talked little, and spent much time outdoors or in solitude. Some, not wishing to involve themselves in the emotional displays of criticism and condemnation, simply watched and departed, allowing their peace to return to them. It was also obvious that there was the emergence of some very healthy bonding and nurturing between the Native American participants.

It was a great conference. It was fun and insightful, provocative and revealing. It was an open portrayal and reflection of all the factions of two opposite cultures that continue to collide, often with substantial coveting and anguish, on both sides.

*   *   *   *   *

But what was I to do with the visions that were being shown to me? Was I to ignore them or pretend they didn't happen? Should I give back what had been freely given to me, just because I am not an Indian? There are no longer any Indians living on this sacred land. The Utes were driven out almost a hundred years ago. There was no longer anyone to ask. No one who knew the sacred places and the ancient legends. There was no one who honored the sacred valley with heartfelt pagan ceremony. At least no one that I had met. The only Ute shaman that I had encountered wanted my total departure and demise, not necessarily in that order. The Source insisted that these were my own personal experiences and I needed to go through my own machinations to sort them out; in this way the most productive learning would be gained.

And so I began to wonder, where did these people that we like to call Indians come from? Who are these people who came and made their claim to this land? If one looks carefully, one can see a wide range of sizes, shapes, facial features, and coloring. Their cultures consisted of highly organized metropolitan cities as well as simple hunting and gathering societies. Great empires rose and fell long before the Europeans ever began "invading" the Americas. Many cultural battles were waged, won and lost long before the more comtemporary European migrations.

According to modern prehistorians and anthropologists, many Indians came from Asia over the land bridges of the Bering Straits by way of Alaska. There has also been a discovery that there were ancient expeditions and colonies from China along the coast of what we now call California. And the Source claimed that small Nordic bands have been migrating from Europe over the seas to America for thousands of years.

Without question, the native peoples of America have endured and continue to endure much at the hands of ignorance and greed. However, they are not immune to contracting bigotry and ignorance just because they are Native Americans. I was learning what the Indians meant when they called someone an apple. That's someone who is red on the outside, but white on the inside. I was also learning what it means to be white on the outside, but red on the inside. It most often means there is no place for you.

It seems to me that many generations ago the white races must have somehow forgotten their own pagan roots. Slowly, cut off from the earth and losing connection with the natural environment, we have evolved into a culture that for the most part is unable or unwilling to understand or grasp the way of the American Indian.

Some of these Native American writers were beginning to publicly demonstrate their assimilation into the dominant culture. They were beginning to travel down their own road to forgetfulness. It is not the people that make the land sacred. It is the land that is sacred. The people come alive when they are able to recognize their mother and learn to honor her and their clans in sacred ways. The magic in the people comes from the land. The magic in the land is the Creator, the true parent of us all. But these conference participants were not necessarily mystics or shaman. They were what the program said they were—Native American writers. They struggle with many of the same challenges as their other American brothers and sisters. They have both the blessing and the burden of attempting to retain and reconnect their teachings and culture within the explosion of an increasingly complex and frenzied technological age.

I realized that much of my reaction and that of some of the audience had the same source. It was not what the writers said that was troubling. It was the fact that many of the Indians had refused to accept whites into their circle. In fact, the philosophy and motivation of several of the participants required that white folks remain outside the circle as an unintelligible, nonredeemable enemy. With a dominant culture replete with vile and blasphemous enemies, spiritually blind and unworthy of sacred things, they can protectively cling to the shards of the shattered vessels that once held and nourished their pagan cultures, cultures that may be mourned for generations to come, cultures that can only be revived if they stay close to the sky, close to the heart, close to the earth.

However, among the insults hurling forth from the tormented souls of that day; one voice remained ringing in my ears. It was piercing and stinging. I was unable to shake free of it, for it was true. I can still hear the voice of a confident young Navajo with the worn old eagle feather and his pronouncement: "We are not your saviours!"

Yes, it was true. Many white people do go to Indians, often like moths to the flame. They are looking for their salvation, their redemption, for they often recognize that pagan peoples have something that they have lost, something they cannot find within themselves, something that has been cauterized from our culture. Many of us long for something sacred. We long to belong to something that is alive, ancient, and forever unfolding and growing.

Yes, it was true. Many of my generation had spent much of their lives trying to be like Indians, whether from America or from India. The quest was the same: searching for a vision, a connection with something sacred; searching for something that had been long ago hidden or forgotten, something that calls to us from the depth of our being, something that demands expression and recognition. This something familiar often haunts us. It is something that we usually have a hard time expressing. Some of us dive into anything hoping some of it might stick to us like some compassionate glue that will hold our tattered lives together.

Others run from the painful haunting, desperately hoping to prove by their self-defiling lifestyles and actions that there isn't anything sacred anywhere. But we remain haunted just the same. For many of us there is still that something that we vaguely recognize and long to know more about. Since it has been lost, many are compelled to search for it in the faces of others where the communion with sacredness still glimmers and glows.

However, I was coming to believe that the white races of this time and age shall not truly be welcome within any pagan circle until their own pagan teachings are reclaimed, treasured, and shared. I was coming to see that all peoples need to rediscover, in each generation, how to return to the circle with quiet dignity, humble knowing, and a respect for the many ways that form the one way of the circle.

Too often we come with arrogance, ignorance, greed, anger, shame, and dependency. This can only be overcome through the kind of love and trust that comes with the personal connection of knowing the source and purpose of one's own being. There are as many ways as there are people. But without one's own story, without one's own link to one's own spiritual heritage, there is only uncertainty and emptiness. It produces a kind of fear and a guarded defensiveness that battles with all that comes within its path.

I became convinced that if there are any white pagan teachings, they need to be found, resurrected, and brought back to life. If we bring power to power, we are strong. If we bring emptiness to power, seeds of emptiness will continue to blossom into covetousness, anger, defilement, and shame. We tend to destroy what we believe we cannot have. We will not tolerate that which we are unable or unwilling to understand.

After the encounter with the Native American writers I was seeing the issues quite clearly. But I also came away with a haunting fear and an uneasiness. I had to accept the possibility that perhaps there are no earth-centered pagan traditions for the white races. If there were any, perhaps they are lost forever. Perhaps it is too late for us. Perhaps there was never anything there.

Meanwhile, I pray we are not witnessing the last vestiges of such connections and teachings within the dwindling communities of our red brothers and sisters. I pray we are not going to render sacred ways of living and being to sterile museums and art galleries where sacredness comes with a certificate of authenticity and can only be afforded by the wealthy.

Nevertheless, I came to realize that there was one essential and overriding message from my visionary experience. Ancient ways can be brought back and made to live once more. And you didn't have to be an Indian to understand. You could experience, comprehend and know, even if the Indians weren't willing or able to understand or to teach you.

I am not forgetting that many souls have their own individualized paths and experiences as they weave back and forth between races and cultures throughout time. The Source has made it abundantly clear that many slaughtered Indians have returned in white bodies. It also claims that many marauding whites have returned in the bodies and communities of impoverished and desolate Indians in order to reap what they have sown. There are many whites who feel and know sacredness. Many Indians are embarrassed by and harass and poke fun at the superstitions that hold their people back from sufficiently utilizing their lands for material gain. They long to move into the mainstream and raise their standard of living to that of our modern technocracy. Before long, some of these tribes may surpass us because they are beginning to discover a balance between the two worlds, the best of both worlds.

Regardless of philosophies of reincarnation, I was also coming to realize that race, genetics, and heritage do matter. Races have history and culture. Like individuals, races have things to learn, and things to remember. There are scores to settle, and there is healing to be done. There are bridges to be built where brave warriors can once again learn the sacred art of battle: how to be strong enough, to be relentless enough in the adherence to the principles of sacred teachings; how to allow ourselves to become vulnerable enough and trusting enough to withstand the fury of betrayal and draw out the tearful bliss of a newfound forgiveness and a rediscovered identity and unity.

I was coming to see that the waywardness of this time and culture could only be resurrected through its own sacred teachings and rememberings. It seems that the white tribes have long ago become ashamed of their earth temples and fearful of wild pagan passions and sacred ways of knowing, labeling them heathen and demonic.

Perhaps our empty Grail can yet be refilled by the nectar of our own gods and goddesses. It seems there needs to be acknowledgment that this generation shall not be answered until it can somehow rediscover its own pagan roots and heritage and blend it into a new, ever-evolving circle of god-filled life.

Yet, once again with this realization, I continued to linger in the subtle terror that perhaps my people never had earth-based, pagan traditions. All I knew of my ancestors is that they came from hordes of shameful Barbarians, Berzerkers, and Vandals. After being conquered by a Holy Roman Empire, we had been saved by the grace of a new age evangelical religion. It had sprung from a cultural heritage that originated somewhere in the Middle East, the home of Armageddon. We then spent a few hundred years being either knights of the roundtable or serfs and slaves. Eventually, we had somehow become cultured and sophisticated.

Once this historical view had been enough. Now, although comforting and familiar, this belief system regarding my heritage was beginning to feel alien. It no longer had the answers that this hungry soul was craving. There had to be more to the story. But it was not clear where or how the answers could be found.

⋆   ⋆   ⋆   ⋆   ⋆

Pondering these things, I walked into the evening darkness through the town park to the little waterfall on Bear Creek. I recalled the rhythm of the beat that had been showered upon me in the vision. I once again wondered if the jaguar experience was real. And, once again, I felt the sweet warm breath upon my neck and the contented purring of my ancient guardian and friend, a guardian of my inner being, a guardian of a very ancient and sacred way.

Whatever my thoughts or conclusions might be, there had erupted this one validating truth. There was being established an ancient and intimate bridge to something that was very sacred. It had reached out to me … and I had become more alive. I was on to something. Perhaps this would become the way. Perhaps this would be the bridge to my own ancestral heritage and my personal quest for redemption.

Chapter Eleven

An Angel?

It was late fall. Indian Summer had given way to several short snow flurries that blustered down from the peaks. After a day or two of melting, the cold had returned. The wind was tormented and howling. It was the kind of wind that makes you want to pull your shoulders up around your ears and shove your fists deep into your pockets. I was frustrated and irritable. It seemed that the more intimate I became with the mountain, and the more familiar I was becoming with its secrets, the more the world was stampeding into this holy citadel, gleefully defiling the sacred promontory. The valley seemed to have become a place where the world came to relieve itself. The stench of greed and debauchery was beginning to permeate the entire region. The grotesque onslaught was relentlessly invading my own consciousness and my own version of how things should be.

Everything bothered me. My wife was becoming entrenched in no-win school board politics. My live-in mother-in-law was beginning to have early bouts of Alzheimer's. But somehow she was only forgetting what was convenient. The kids were fighting. The dog ran off … so I decided I'd run off too.

After tearing through the bedroom closet in quest of my most experienced pair of hiking boots, I grabbed my pack and headed up the mountain. Most of the leaves were gone. The sky was lifeless and gray. The grass was brown and withered. If the sun had risen, I couldn't find it. It was hunting season, but I wasn't carrying a rifle. I was wearing my old military field jacket. I tied several streamers of orange engineering tape to the epaulets— just in case someone thought I looked like a deer wearing a blue backpack and an orange stocking cap.

The ground felt strange. On the surface, the mud was hard and frozen. Just beneath the surface there were places where the earth was still soft and warm. It was kind of like walking on expensive carpeting with thick padding. It placed an unnatural spring in my step. Meandering along, I braced against the occasional gusts of frigid air that stung my nose and numbed my cheeks. Stomping onward, my irritability began to transform itself into a monotonous two-step dance accompanied by the responsive beating of my heart. Soon small beads of perspiration began to trickle down my face and neck. Tugging on the zipper, I opened the jacket so as not to get too overheated. Too much perspiration can lead to hypothermia when cold winds blow.

I traveled west along the south-facing slope, steadily moving upward in elevation. After several hundred yards, I left the abandoned Jeep road and followed an obscure game trail that eventually led into a gnarled thicket of dense oak brush. While stumbling over a loose rock, I slammed my forehead into the rough bark of a twisted oak. Falling to my knees, I found myself cursing at the pain and wondering why I had left the easier path behind. Swatting at the twigs and branches around me, I struggled back to my feet, regained my composure, and climbed out of the thicket. Without a path, walking slowly, my eyes were focused downward toward the loose and unstable ground.

Suddenly the air exploded with the throbbing pulse of powerfully beating wings. My head jerked back. I was looking directly into two huge round eyes that were on a collision course with my nose. Before I could blink, a terrifying screech filled my alarmed ears. A wing tip brushed against my shoulder as the bird catapulted by my face. It was a magnificently raging white owl with black and gray markings. My heart thundered. My stomach imploded. My knees weakened. I don't know which was the most startling, the suddenness of its point blank appearance, or the majesty of its beauty, power, and speed.

Standing awestruck, mind and emotions became riveted and tranquil. Thought became enlivened awareness. Weariness became fullness. Frustration became conviction. There remained a cautious part of me that felt like it had received some kind of warning. However, a more assuring part of me experienced the event as a welcome challenge; manifesting as a wake-up call, demanding my attention, helping me to reclaim my spiritual resolve. The journey continued across the escarpment and into a large stand of aspen.

The strength and power of the wind began to build. It became very dramatic and expressive. The howling and moaning pushed and shoved, coaxed and teased, hid for a while, then exploded with a tantrum of fierceness. It began pulling, drawing, swirling, gusting into every crevice of my being. As a close friend once described it, these are the kinds of winds that come from the breath of the Creator. It was the kind of wind that reminds you that there is more going on than what can be seen by the eye. It was the kind of wind that blows away all the impurities and stimulates inner knowing and inspiration. This was the force that began to massage my every thought and emotion. Then they were thrown back into my face with the subtlety and playfulness of an out-of-control forest fire; a fire, fanned by sacred, wings that purges the landscape in any direction and in any manner it chooses.

A frenzied squall thundered upon the scene with a torrent of swirling dead leaves and loose twisted grass. Acknowledging the presence of power, the trees began to sway and rock in unison. I noticed that some of the aspen looked like they were going to fall. A part of me, fearing for safety, wanted to panic. However, nature's display was so empowering and stimulating that I didn't want to squander this experience on such a feeble and unproductive emotion. So I just stood my ground, watched, and absorbed the raw passion that was unraveling before me.

Trees that had grown closely huddled together seemed to be able to endure the fury better than those that were stranded and alone. Most of the damage was being done to trees that were sick and dying, or growing in places where the roots had little support. Many of the floundering trees were decayed and brittle. The sap had stopped flowing long ago. They were no longer able to anchor themselves into the rich nourishing earth that sends towering trees groping into the restless oceans of air.

The raging tempest tugged at the rattling forest and exposed roots that had become rigid and unyielding, no longer able to flex and bend. Unlike their healthy brethren, they had forgotten how to dance in cadence with the prancing winds. Inevitably, rotting wood began to crack and split. Several lifeless stalks groaned, twisted, and bowed precariously before clumsily collapsing onto the forest floor. Shattered remnants of amputated branches cascaded downward, coming to rest right in front of me, scattering themselves helplessly across the frozen path. I began to watch the tree line a little nervously as I realized how close the fallen trees had come to where I stood.

Standing at the middle of the squall, I took a few moments to regain my breath and to restore my composure. As I continued up the ridge, the intensity of the wind eventually began to subside. Approaching an open meadow, I experienced a sense of relief and lifted my hand to shade my eyes from the harshness of a sun that was beginning to emerge from the clouded horizon. As I bit into a cold crisp apple, the radiant sun began to warm my face and hands.

Methodically surveying the terrain, I discovered a parked vehicle sitting to one side of the clearing. The road had become a rutted trail that had all but vanished from disuse. It was a pickup camper that was at least fifteen years old. There were fresh scratches on one side from battling through tree branches and oak brush. It sported new tires with raised white letters. The vehicle appeared to be well maintained.

I almost missed a fragile-looking old man sitting motionlessly on the passenger side, peering at me through the window. Responding to my presence, he opened the door, stepped out of the truck, and laid a rifle across the seat. His eyes were a rich blue and his hair was completely white. He was very well groomed. His skin had the look of a man who didn't spend much time outdoors. He seemed very familiar, but I couldn't recall where we had previously met.

After a friendly greeting, he explained that the younger members of his party were taking a walk up the ridge to see if they could fill their deer licenses. Apparently, he had decided to stay out of the cold wind and remained in the pickup. After a brief exchange of clichés, I excused myself and continued into the forest and on up the mountain. As I looked back over my shoulder, he climbed back into the truck.

The wooded foothills were full of patches of snow that had been left in the frigid shadows. The leaves were crisp and brittle and would not permit quiet stalking. The snow patches crunched beneath my boots like large flat pieces of cracking styrofoam. Aspen became interspersed with evergreens. A few remaining birds chirped and bounced in the tree tops, casting dancing shadows across intermittent rays of warming sunlight. Walking onward, I decided I would meet up with the Sheep Creek Trail and traverse back toward town, completing the tour in one large oval-shaped circle.

The ground was not as steep as it had been. It was almost flat in some places. This afforded the opportunity to get my own wind back. Enjoying the excursion, I began chanting a version of a sita ram mantra and pretended that I was singing to the sleeping plants and trees. A startled young deer bolted from a ravine to my right and ran down the other side of the trail. I wondered if there would be gunshots from the hunters. It was headed in that direction.

There was one last push up steep terrain to reach the Forest Service trail. It had once been used by pack animals and mule trains—blazed through pristine wilderness by old-timers who are now forgotten. Panting and lunging, I finally claimed the top of an eighty- or ninety-foot ridge. It jutted out, right next to the deteriorating trail that I was seeking. To my amazement, I found my elderly acquaintance resting upon the stump of a fallen tree. I wanted to be alone, but he had caught my interest. So I decided to talk to him once again.

I crunched toward him through the brittle snow. I found myself feeling a little self-conscious and wondered if he had heard my chanting. As I approached him, he said he enjoyed my singing and told me that a lot of people came up here to sing. Although a bit wrinkled, his skin seemed to be very soft and smooth. Its appearance was almost unblemished and had a translucent quality. His eyes were remarkably clear and bright. However, every time I made eye contact, I seemed to forget what I was thinking or saying.

This was a very elderly but obviously vibrant person. I was puzzled as to how he was able to pass by unnoticed and reach my destination before I did. But I seemed too perplexed to ask the question. He asked if I had seen any big bucks. I said no and explained that I wasn't a deer hunter. He then acknowledged that I wasn't carrying a weapon. I remember him saying how a lot of people come hunting in the mountains but are unable to recognize what they are looking for, even after they find it. After a few moments of comfortable silence, we mutually acknowledged our love of the mountains. A wave of restlessness washed over me, and I found myself returning to the trail.

Almost immediately I became riddled with curiosity. Who was this guy? How did he get by me? What was his name? Where did he come from? (Did he want to buy real estate?) Turning around, I returned to the ridge and retraced my steps in the softening snow. However, he was already gone.

Then I made a startling discovery. He had left no footprints in the snow. I could see my own footprints. I could see my original approach. I could see where I had left and returned. On the precise top of the narrow ridge there was no snow. There were several spots where the snow had melted. However, the entire area was ringed with snow. You could not approach our meeting place without crossing snow. There was no evidence that this gentleman I had talked to had ever been there. I resumed the chant and sauntered back through the forest and into the valley.

Later that evening while talking to my wife, I mentioned the interesting gentleman that I had met on my hike. I went on to remark how surprised I had been that a supposedly feeble old man had been able to somehow pass by me undetected and meet me at my undisclosed destination. He seemed to be so familiar, yet I still could not recall where I had seen him.

The channel became engaged. The Source informed me that this was a celestial being from another dimension. This *was* an old friend. He had not necessarily come there just to see me, but he had given me his blessing. He was merely visiting the mountain in the same way that I was a visitor. As I approached, he took advantage of the existing truck and portrayed himself as a hunter. He was apparently not sure how I would respond to his presence.

I was told that if another person would have been there, they would not have seen him. It was explained that my perception was due to the heightened level of consciousness brought about by the power of the mountain and other uncommon circumstances. I was told that these were the kinds of experiences that the Source hopeed I would continue to encounter in my quest for things of a spiritual nature. These experiences tend to remove doubt and expand our limited intellectual capacities in ways that are not easily understood by the conscious mind. It was suggested that I should have recognized the gentleman, for I had met him before, sitting with his bicycle, meditating with me, along the Old Spanish Trail in Tucson.

The owl was supposedly real. It had come to symbolically challenge the worthiness of a venture into a hidden realm of the sacred citadel. I was told that the test was passed.

Within this strange and ever-evolving pilgrimage into the mountain, this event had become another landmark into an ever-expanding way of seeing, hearing, and being. Another door had been opened to a place that I had always believed to exist only within the confines of imagination, symbolic myth, and speculation.

If it were possible to commune with kachinas, why wouldn't it be possible to commune with angelic beings? My beleaguered mind continued to struggle with the things it had witnessed, and questioned the validity, the purpose, and the implications of all that was being experienced upon the mountain. It all seemed something too far removed from traditional logic. Abstract spiritual concepts were becoming a bit too real for comfort.

I still find myself contemplating the experiences of that day. I find myself wondering about what is real and what is hidden right in front of our noses; what miracles we miss as we plod along within our daily tasks when we don't take the time to stop, to look, and to see.

Chapter Twelve

The Hystory of a Quest

M om and Dad discovered Telluride in 1955 when a friend encouraged them to take a vacation to southwestern Colorado. Although somewhat successful, you could always sense that Dad had a restless nature that was in quest of something better, something a little closer to wilderness, something somewhere out West. There had been an earlier attempt to free himself from the Midwest when we moved to Williams, Arizona. He built a cabin a few miles north of town and had a couple of memorable years developing a flagstone quarry. But it became necessary to return to Iowa to take care of the family business after Granddad had a heart attack.

As a pilot, Dad chartered occasional private excursions for sportsmen. He enjoyed many hunting and fishing trips in the West and into the Canadian wilderness. There were occasional opportunities to visit some very remote locations. However, after a single visit to Telluride, he announced that this was where we were going to live. Although he later lived in other places, his home was always in Telluride. He had hoped to somehow utilize his studies in mining engineering to make a living through mineral exploration and development. Becoming a small mine and mill operator had always been his dream.

Dad was mesmerized by the power and beauty of the mountains. For decades, he intermittently scoured the high country seeking to find his fortune. As every hard rock miner knows, ore follows veins that can sometimes run for miles through the undulating metamorphic and igneous rock formations. There are places where these thickened veins collide and induce a massive concentration of precious metals that old-timers sometimes call

145

the mother lode. Dad had always hoped that he could locate one of those special places where these veins would come together in a profusion of mineral activity.

He was realistic and knew that finding such a place was a long shot, but he couldn't stop thinking about it and trying to make it happen. He would have been happy to have had a simple little mill that would run a few tons of ore per day and eke out a seasonal living, retreating from the high country during the long winters. But, like Oscar, he could never quite let go of the dream—the possibility of locating that elusive chamber of riches. He was happiest when he was full of the passion of being just one step behind, but rapidly closing in on, the discovery of that one point where the many veins would merge.

Flying a Cessna over the peaks and through the basins, he could trace the exposed red, orange, and yellow leaching that bears witness to the presence of rich mineral-bearing ore. With the eye of an eagle, he would search for that special place he just knew had to be there, somewhere within the mountain. I still remember him rising before the sun, spending hours studying and memorizing books, journals, and old coffee-stained maps, trying to locate that overlooked vein that would point the way to pay dirt. He used to joke that he had mining claims worth over ten million dollars, but it would take twenty million to get the ore out. In later years he came to believe that the center he searched for was located deep beneath one of the high alpine volcanoes that had become a lake.

In pursuit of Dad's quest, we would sometimes visit Jimmy Noyes, who referred to himself as the mayor of Ophir. Jimmy had a habit of encouraging his "pet" skunks to come by for a few table scraps toward the end of the day in the early evening twilight. This sometimes made visitors a little uncomfortable. He always claimed that they never caused any problems, but I must admit I was never fully convinced.

At that time, Mr. Noyes and a female friend were the last year-round residents in what was left of the town. Although he was still quite active, he was obviously failing. The middle-aged lady had befriended the mayor and was serving as companion, cook, nurse, and housekeeper. This arrangement seemed to cause a bit of a stir in some people's minds. However, from my point of view it had seemed to be a very practical arrangement. Jimmy was fortunate to find someone so willing and able to make his last years a little more comfortable.

In the early sixties, Mr. Noyes was at least eighty years old. In his youth he had once worked with the mule trains that would go into the high alpine basins and pack ore back down into the valley for custom milling. This was a way that miners with small claims could get their ore milled without a huge investment in machinery. Jimmy had an excellent opportunity to know the type and quality of ore that had come out of the Ophir side of the mountain. This was of particular interest to my father, who liked to search Jimmy's memories for clues to the mineral secrets of the mountains. Sitting in a creaking rocking chair beside a warm wood-burning stove, quietly slurping hot tea, was a living, breathing piece of history. Wiping a trickle of tea from his unshaven chin, he would reach deep into the past and share his life with us. He used to tell marvelous stories. He claimed to be able to remember things in the Ophir valley back when he was only five or six years old.

During one visit he showed us an old black book. It was dusty and worn. Jimmy held the book as if it were sacred scripture. He would occasionally rub on the cover with his forearm and shirt sleeve. After a long period of silence, he held it out to my father and told him he thought he might find it useful. It was a book of dreaming, hoping, and finding. It provided a record of mining claim locations and assay information of various claims and mines in the region. It also included some basic information regarding mining law. It was an attempt at putting together a directory of all the active mining claims in the region. Published in 1883, it had been sponsored by advertisers, obviously hoping to inspire gold and silver seekers who would then buy more mining and milling equipment. I still have the book and treasure the notes and references that Dad left in the margins.

Dad returned to the mountain in the spring of 1978 and set up camp next to the river. While he was dying from cancer, he left a record of his thoughts and hopes. It was left in a place where he knew I would find it—inside the book. It wasn't so much what he had found but what had been learned and experienced as he shared his life and dreams. My relationship with him was all the more special because, despite some youthful indiscretions, he had made a conscious decision to acknowledge me as his biological son, marry my mother, and share with us his life and heritage. The book is a sacred object of our time together upon the mountain in quest of something very tangible, but sometimes difficult to explain.

Now, I had returned to the San Juan mine at a place called Matterhorn near Priest Lake. It was the place where he had set up his mill so many years before. It was built in a time when the paved highway that now runs by it was only a rutted dirt road. The cabin had been dismantled and traded for labor. All traces of it were gone, but I could still see the little flattened area where Dad had planted a small garden almost thirty years before.

The building that housed the mill had been made of used lumber recycled from an old barn near the town of Norwood. A few timbers had been salvaged from an abandoned narrow gauge railroad trestle. The milling equipment and other machinery had been removed in the late sixties. The primitive structure had collapsed from thirty years of heavy winter snows. Most of the remaining wood was soft and rotting. A few mushrooms grew between the insect infested planks that had once been a roof. Several flourishing trees had sprouted and stretched upward from the dirt floor of the disintegrating building.

This had been a very wet spring. Green grass was thick and tall. Wildflowers were in abundance. Our children ran along the aspen-covered hillside, exploring, laughing, giggling, and squabbling. It was a great day for a picnic. My wife spread out the four corners of an old Army blanket that had once been used on one of the old military cots in the cabin.

We sat beneath a lone blue spruce that was about twenty feet tall. It was the same blue spruce that Dad had planted next to the cabin door. The same tree that he used to talk to as he smoked his morning cigarette. As we unpacked our lunch, I began to remember. This was the place where I had spent most of my summers. This was the place that Dad called base camp. He had hoped to haul high grade ore from the high country during the summer and do some milling during the winter. He had hoped the ore from the San Juan mine would be able to pay expenses. I remembered my mother coming out from town on the weekends bringing fresh supplies and her latest batch of homemade bread.

When you live in Telluride, you seem to have a lot of visitors. This was true even back then. Some of them we hardly knew, but they seemed convinced that we were great friends. Dad understood why they were there. They too were drawn to the grandeur of the mountain. A few of the people that visited were very welcome and very much missed after they left.

I remember one year when my mother's parents visited. I believe it was in the fall. I was off working with the men doing something that seemed terribly important while the womenfolk remained in the cabin. It was cold and snowing. I had gotten wet and was getting sick and feverish. Of course, a strong young mountain lad like myself wasn't about to complain or mention any discomfort, especially when I was trying to show my Granddad how grown up I had become. This Granddad had worked hard most of his life and had become a construction foreman at the age of sixteen. I wasn't about to do him dishonor by wimping out. However, when we returned to the one-room cabin, my grandmother knew at a glance what the situation was and what to do.

Without hesitation, she sat me down in front of the wood-burning kitchen stove and immediately took off my wet boots and socks. She presented me with a pair of dry pants and draped one of the Army surplus blankets around my shivering shoulders. She was able to do all of this with an absolute economy of words. She was able to accomplish this feat without any ruffling of a budding male ego. In a couple of minutes there was hot chocolate and an insightful tale about what had once happened to her when she was a young girl on the farm. Sometimes she would tell me about her parents, but I didn't pay much attention. She would talk about how her kinfolk on both sides of the family had come to live in the Midwest around 1840 to 1860. She could trace her ancestors back to places like Wendon, Pomerania, and Scandia.

My grandmother was a lady with considerable talent and perseverance. She had raised five children on a farm during the Depression. She came from a time and a place where children and family were the proper focus of a woman's attention. I know it is no longer politically correct to see that as a woman's role. And although we may say that it is all right if a woman chooses that role, most people no longer acknowledge or respect a woman who dedicates herself to those things. Women of this caliber are usually seen as not being able or willing to have a real career. They are often seen as coming from an unenlightened age when they were still enslaved by their ruthless male oppressors. It was clear to anyone who knew them that Granddad couldn't have made it without her.

This was a special kind of woman who knew how to make a garden produce fun as well as food. In retirement, she raised two grandchildren and started a home drapery business. She taught Granddad how to sew and hang drapes almost as well as she could. This was a woman who knew the value of a well-honed axe. Before she left town, she had secretly cut a half cord of paper-thin kindling. As she left, she told me this was my Christmas present because that's when I would appreciate it the most. The warmth of her fire still blazes brightly within my heart and soul.

This was just one of dozens of special memories brought into focus by a family pilgrimage to a place where my father had planted his dreams.

My son began pulling at an old rusting pipe that had been wedged into some rocks in an embankment. A small stream of water still trickled out of the pipe and dribbled into an overflowing puddle lined with flat rocks. This was where we got the water for washing and gardening. My daughter was admiring a cluster of blossoming columbines next to the trio of aspens where I had erected a tree house. The trunk of the tree was still scarred where I had carved my initials when I was eleven years old. As Winchester enthusiastically scampered around her, she quietly explored her grandfather's legacy.

I hadn't had any particular interest in guns or hunting since my discharge from the Army. However, on that day I decided that in two or three years I would return to this place with my children and teach them, as my father had taught me, the appropriate use of firearms. I would tell them the story of how the deer had been taken that stood just beyond the cabin door. I would tell them the story of Oscar and the white elk and hope that they might recognize the difference between being a sportsman and being a hunter.

I made a few awkward attempts at explaining to my children what I was remembering. However, I mostly got blank stares and distracted nods. These were my memories, not theirs.

They were here to make memories of their own. My memories and my children's memories will not be the same. However, there will be some very special places where the edges of these memories merge together and weave the tapestry of the generations.

After lunch we stretched out on the blanket and enjoyed the cool breezes that were gently rising and falling with the rattling of aspen leaves. We may have even drifted off to sleep for a few moments. After we had rested, I tied a prayer feather to Dad's spruce and took the hand of the one who had become my friend, lover, and partner. We began walking along the overgrown path that had once been a haulage road built to bring treasure out of the mountain. The children scurried behind, running, walking, and exploring. I knew from the tone of the voice and the look in the eyes that the Source was about to speak. The one God of an ancient priestess was about to impart sacred knowledge. Another lesson was to be given.

To my surprise, the Source did not impart. It began asking questions, drawing out of my own restless consciousness what it was that was troubling; what it was that was being experienced; what it was that was being sought. I was perplexed and more than a little irritated. If the Source had something to say, why didn't it just say it? Why string things out with a cat and mouse game? However, it was made clear that the exercise that was being offered was for the purpose of continuing to learn to pull from my own consciousness and not "to always be spoon fed like a helpless little child."

The mountain had once again been calling, throughout my dreaming and even into my waking. My own version of the mother lode was being revealed. I had been shown images of glowing energy lines flowing into and out of the sacred promontories. Crossing and tracing some of these areas on various walks and hikes, I could feel waves of heat, energy, and sometimes gut-wrenching turmoil. These meridians ran into and through three primary energy points within the region that formed one unified beacon that sometimes shines and glimmers and forms a bridge between the physical and ethereal realms. At times these sanctified conclaves felt as if they were being placed under massive attack by a host of angry energies, raging with the anguish of vicious betrayal.

There had been a series of dreams peering across and into the time and space of an epic story that had become absorbed into the mountains. At times it was as if one could see and feel the collective manifestation of all the thoughts, hopes, and dreams of the generations of pilgrims that migrated into the region.

This would be a day of wondering and contemplation. This would be a day of realization and discovery. Ancient teachings born of ancient knowing were being suspected, recognized, and confirmed. Ancient knowing was drawing one of its children back to the mountain. Ancient teachings were clamoring for rebirth and resurrection. With a little coaxing they began pushing their heads out of the warm moist soil and were brought into the sunlight where they would be caressed and nurtured by gentle breezes.

Continuing slowly along the trail, the litany of thoughts, images, and experiences began to come into focus and were carefully examined. The more I was questioned, the clearer things became, the more there was to see.

Just a few hundred years ago waves of European explorers, adventurers, and pilgrims began charging across the American continents. They usually came with a conviction that they held an absolute sovereignty, usually claiming to have conquered and possessed all that they could see and grasp.

Mariners in leaking, wooden, wind-powered boats ventured into a seemingly endless and unchartable ocean. They faced devastating gales, mutiny, starvation, and death. They braved a fear-based mythology that propagated the possibility of demons, devils, sea serpents, and unholy hexes and curses. Once reaching an unfamiliar shore, they might encounter hidden reefs, unknown pestilence and hostile natives. They might have to struggle through an alien and inhospitable wilderness hoping to replenish diminished provisions. They might even become stranded or marooned, never again to see their homeland. Conquistadors, forsaking their homes and families, searched thousands of miles on foot and horseback, enduring humid and hostile jungles, dry baking deserts with cracked parched earth, and treacherous mountain passes howling with the stinging cold of blinding blizzards.

Once the foothold was established, the clouded dream raged on in a proud and arrogant proclamation of manifest destiny. To their way of thinking, they had a God-given mandate to conquer and build a nation out of an inhospitable, heathen wilderness, leveling forests, harnessing rivers, creating farms, building railroads, homes and factories.

Through the inner vision, I was experiencing ephemeral visages of holy men and sacred women making pilgrimage to great temples of energy and light, dancing and chanting with thundering drums; long lazy summers, rich and bountiful, with brown-faced warriors cuddling with wild-women warriors giving birth to the children of the earth clans; columns and scattered bands of weary emaciated conquistadors encased in iron, willing themselves forward, in quest of cities of gold, power and glory; monks and priests in search of a bountiful harvest of conquerable souls and rebukable demons; wild and roaming half-crazed explorers and trappers lost in a wilderness sea of their own pagan reflections and machinations; swarms of meandering prospectors drawn onward into the mountains, driven by dreams of adventure, wealth and freedom; tents, shanties, cabins, boarding houses, bawdy houses, saloons, and mill sites springing up like mushrooms, and then merging back into pulsating, moaning earth.

Eventually, an isolated and forgotten little village emerges, quietly nestled into an ancient and sacred valley. Finally, there is the arrival of my family, cast into a brief but treasured page of the growing history of these shining mountains.

Now appearing within the mind's eye are harried waves of unsynchronized random thought forms, battling and struggling to take on color and form, sometimes vibrant and shimmering, sometimes putrid; expansive images of resort complexes crowding upon treeless slopes, covering mesas within a raging specter of writhing and seething shadows; all manifesting as a rapidly advancing glacier of never complete but ever evolving architectural patterns that ooze along the Telluride Valley floor and up into the hillsides and up onto the mesas. Meanwhile, a once wild and free river, choking with steel and concrete chains, withers and falls into a moaning fire filled chasm, belching forth the stench of toxic steam, while stranded fish rotting on dry cracked clay are gobbled up by frantic and starving scavengers that stampede into darkened caverns where they lay expended from their writhing death dance, poisoned and ashamed.

All these thoughts, feelings and images seemed to hover precariously over the land in some unseen spirit world, clamoring and demanding in one massive unrestrained fit of wailing to rip the silent veil asunder in order to herald their birth into an earthly manifestation that smothers sacred ground.

We were bearing witness to the later stages of a continuing saga of the largest migration of people and culture that had ever been experienced upon this planet.

All of these are in quest of something a little different, something special, something that holds the promise of things sacred and fulfilling. They are often in quest of an outwardly visible sign or symbol that represents an invisible psychological and spiritual reality. Each wave synthesizing its goal into a vision that fans imagination, hope and determination. For some it was freedom of worship; for others it was free land and hidden riches. For some it is something much more. All were called by the halcyon cry, summoned by the hungry haunting lodged deep within their souls.

All of those responding to the calling came with a myriad of ideas about how things should be and what was possible. Each wave and each generation came with its own out-of-focus vision of what the land of milk and honey should become, often unable to recognize what was right before them.

Wise elders sometimes tell us that, in order to have a great learning, there must be a vision that inspires action and commitment. If the vision is not born of truth and righteousness, it will end in holocaust. Yet, from the ashes of each holocaust brought about through the lack of wisdom, compassion and, connectedness, comes the opportunity for reassessment, learning, redefining, and committing to a purer version of the vision. Each generation has the renewed opportunity to refocus the vision, to see it more clearly and to hear and to yield to the sweet melody of songs that are eternally sacred.

In answering the call to seize the promised land, they are in fact responding to genetic memory and returning like salmon to the spawning grounds of their soul's own creation. Separated in consciousness from their ancient teachings and driven by a primal lusting to reclaim something that they can no longer name, they are driven by an insatiable hunger for something that is worth risking everything. And all the while, slashing through a multitude of pagan nations and traditions that are depositories of knowledge and wisdom as ancient as the earth itself. All the while, like a madman lost in a parched desert, ravenously lapping up the remaining traces of crystal droplets of water, unaware of the thirst quenching nectar that flows just below the surface of pillaged landscape. With little understanding and even less recognition of sacredness, opposite cultures collide with a howling holocaust that crucifies much more than just the people.

Now, as the revealing begins, some are beginning to see and to feel the great anguish that looms before this generation. Shocked and confused by the great ignorance and the insatiable lust for what they cannot buy or steal, some are beginning to take another look—seeing a little deeper and seeing a little clearer. Some are struggling to wonder what went wrong; what could have been done better; what of value might be salvaged, honored, and cherished.

As they wrestle with the majesty that is the mountain, most have no idea of what is towering before them. They just don't get it. They continue to flounder with the what to do and the how to be. They struggle in desperation to drown out and pave over the uncomfortable rumblings of their pleading souls, yearning for the redemption of the knowing and the sharing of things that are eternally sacred.

They plot and conspire to somehow harness its holiness, beauty, and power in order to serve insatiable schemes of riches and domination. Yet, here and there it seems there is learning. Here and there is enough nurtured knowing to allow new seeds to be born and to prosper. Here and there is the opportunity to commence the resurrection of a people, a race, and a planet. Fortunately, like the salmon, only a few from each generation are needed to claim the goal and to once more bring a new generation of life back to the people.

These were the images, thoughts, and feelings that had been gleaned from intrapsychic and astral realms which were now enshrouding the mental abyss of my driven and tortured soul on that sweet and gentle summer day. It was a day when the veil was lifted for a brief moment and unseen guides spoke from out of a mother priestess and showed me an ancient way of seeing, remembering, and being.

Chapter Thirteen

Wodan's Fire

It was time to make pilgrimage into the high country. A short one-hour hike produced a realization that this was to be a trek of substantial duration. Twice plans were made and then postponed. I needed to be free of worrying about how long and how far. Several days before, I had begun to carefully reorganize my backpack in anticipation of the excursion. Three prayer feathers were prepared for the mini-expedition. There was no particular plan. I knew I was going north into the high alpine basins, far above timberline. There was a sense that I might even go on to the other side. I was determined to take my time and to enjoy the adventure.

There was a commitment to trust that internal compass and to follow it wherever it might lead. I selectively packed a few basic emergency survival items as well as a little food, water, and extra clothing. It is generally considered to be a violation of standard safety precautions to venture into the wilderness alone. I know it isn't very logical, but there has always been a strong feeling that there was nothing in the Telluride mountains that could ever harm me. At any rate, there are times when one must enter the wilderness alone; allowing nothing to distract the connection between the explorer and the explored. This was one of those times.

Tossing my gear into the black and white Jeep, I headed up Tomboy Road and began the first leg of the journey. I hadn't gone very far when I realized that this was an excursion that should be made totally on foot. I needed to feel the earth beneath my feet. It was time to put aside this age of technology and find a parking place for my mechanical steed. Discovering a little extra room on one of the switchbacks, I inched the Jeep into the high bank, backing as far as possible so that the road wouldn't be blocked. A note was left on the windshield explaining my general direction and potential time of return. I pulled the straps of the pack around my shoulders and slammed the poor-fitting metal door. The parking brake was not very reliable. A couple of rocks placed in front of the oversized tires were an added precaution against losing the Jeep over the side of the hill.

Gazing at the sky, I stretched my arms upward and took a long deep cleansing breath. Looking eastward, I allowed my eyes a moment of blissful feasting upon Ajax and Bridal Veil Falls. Turning northward, I bumped into a woman who was standing right next to me.

She immediately apologized. "Pardon me, sir. I didn't mean to startle you."

I was thoroughly annoyed. I didn't like being startled, but I was. I had no idea where she had come from. I didn't see her when I drove up, and I had a hard time admitting that I had been so unaware of my surroundings.

So, although my heart was pounding, I casually replied, "Oh, that's all right. I'm not startled. I knew you were there."

Before I finished my sentence, she informed me that she wanted to go along with me on my hike. That sure took a lot of nerve. To my way of thinking, an excursion into the high country is a very intimate thing and this stranger was intrusively inviting herself along. I was all set, centered, tuned in to the natural beauty. The grand meditation was starting to unfold. Then here comes some inconsiderate flat-lander yuppie forcing her way into my privately planned adventure. I responded abruptly.

"Well, I'm on my way up into the high country, above timberline. That's pretty rough terrain if you're not used to it. Not just anybody can handle it, especially if you're not used to the altitude."

Upon hearing my eruption, I felt brutish and insensitive. I was surprised at how I had lashed out in such a rude and callous manner.

Her skin was exceedingly fair and radiant. Her cheeks were so rosy that they were almost blushing. She had long auburn hair that hung in thick braids, which were meticulously wrapped with long slender strips of rawhide. She had the kind of eyes that a man would gladly become lost in.

She was open and vulnerable. My sarcastic remarks had caught her off guard. They had hit their mark. I could see that she felt a bit awkward and slightly injured. She made no effort to hide or fend off her reaction to my verbal attack. Anyone could see she was a very special woman, and she didn't need to be treated in such an offensive manner.

She wore an off-white blouse with a bit of lace. Her jumper was made of a rich brown woven material. It almost looked homespun. Around the edges her clothing was adorned with a simple gold-colored braid that had highlights of green within the pattern. It was hard to get a fix on her. At times she appeared to be a powerful, wise, and passionate woman. Then she seemed to be a simple trusting child. As we began to walk, she put out her hand. I instinctively took hold of it and steadied her as she stepped around some uneven ground. I thought she said her name was Frita.

At times she seemed very sensual, as if she were a lonely young woman looking for some intimate male companionship. Then I would shake off the thought, judging myself to be grotesquely presumptuous. Her openness and vulnerability served her well. She was seeking reassurance that she really didn't need. It was almost as if she were seeking reassurance in order to make me feel more comfortable. Although I was attracted to her, I really wasn't interested. I was on my way to the peaks. She wasn't prepared for rain, snow, or sleet. She had no food, water, or warm clothing. And as interesting as she may have been, she was a distraction from my quest, even though I wasn't clear about how it might manifest.

If her goal was some romantic companionship, she needed to get the message that I was already taken so she could move on to her next prospect. I was happily committed to my wife and had never found cause to stray. Once again, her openness and vulnerability seemed to cancel out and make a mockery of any lascivious speculation. Yet the speculation somehow lingered.

She explained that she loved flowers and growing things. She proclaimed that she hoped to have the opportunity to watch some mountain seeds sprouting, budding, and blooming. She entreated me to spend the day with her in search of a blossoming meadow. She seemed to know that it was the right season for green growing things in the high country. She had a special interest in finding a certain variety of flower. However, it was unfamiliar to me and I don't remember its name.

I took the lead on the trail. This section was steep and strenuous. Conversation stopped. She lagged behind but did not seem to be particularly fatigued. Coming to more level terrain, I waited for her to catch up. She walked slowly, methodically, gracefully, sometimes stopping and gently stroking the maturing wild berries that crowded portions of the path. When she reached the top of the hill, she walked right up to me, stood very close, and hesitantly placed her hand on my shoulder.

I started to turn away to continue the journey. Once again, she asked if she might join me. Revealing my apprehension, I explained that I was on a spiritual pilgrimage. Although I had planned to make the journey alone, I decided that she was welcome to walk with me as far as she wished. However, she needed to understand that it might be a very strenuous journey, far past timberline. I wasn't sure how long the trip would take.

Acknowledging my concern, she smiled and simply said, "I understand." As we wandered through a little peninsula of aspen trees, she knelt down and began to carefully inspect the ground as she poked at the fertile soil. She stated, "I think I have already found my flower."

There was a whole array of various alpine wildflowers scattered among the aspen. She seemed very pleased. She smiled again, and I returned to the trail. After a few moments I turned to look back. She was gone. There was no trace of her. She had disappeared as abruptly as she had arrived. I didn't think much of it

at the time, thinking she had gone over the edge of the hill following her interest in her flowers. Later on I found myself
wondering about her origin. However, I was mostly wondering if
I were becoming delusional. The Source would later respond,
"You already know the answer." I later came to realize that her
name is Freyja.

I was following a primitive mining road that headed in the
general direction of the San Sophia Range. It was clinging to the
side of the hill and winding through tall evergreen trees. It was
dramatically quiet, the kind of quiet where you can feel the
trees breathing. Each step crunched through the solitude like a
small muffled explosion. As clouds gathered, the forest grew
dark and still. Occasionally, you could hear a falling branch, or
the frenzied scuffle of some small four-footed animal, or the
startled flutter of bird wings. Before long, even these occasional
stirrings were absorbed into the silence. As usual, my feet began
to keep cadence with the pounding of my heart. My body felt
heavy. I began to sweat. Onward I climbed, step after step after
step. My legs and lower back began to ache. It was time to stop,
rest, and enjoy a few ounces of water. I sat down in the middle of
the trail.

Looking between the trees to the southwest, I could see the
ski slopes. The last two summers, there was an almost continuous smoky fog coming off the burning of timber. Slow to
disperse, it would often settle into the valley. The lifeless gray
cast was barely recognizable from the valley floor. Only when you
reached the high ground could you become aware of its impact.
Wide strips of forest were being cut down in order to expand the
resort, to make more ski runs, more roads, sell more lots, and
litter the terrain with more trophy houses.

Person by person, project by project, the growth made
sense—jobs, growth, sharing this inspiring wilderness with others. However, as a whole, the growth was beginning to have the
appearance of an insatiable growing cancer. Each wave of development changed things just a little bit. Each generation of
investors and vacationers would only see their small and

acceptable portion of change and compromise. But when you look at the overall impact to this pristine environment, it is devastating.

The process is as inevitable as the seasons. It is as hard to stop development of these sanctuaries as it is to stop the lion from lusting after the warm flesh of the newborn lamb. It would be easier to hold back the tides of the ocean than to halt the onslaught. What can you say to those who have no concept of anything sacred? What can you say to those who are truly proud of what they are doing and believe that their projects are an improvement?

"My god!" I gasped. I was sounding like the Indians!

Rising to my feet, the cadence of slow monotonous steps resumed. Breathing heavily, legs responding like rubber, it seemed like the climb would never end. I began chanting to myself. My vision narrowed. Mind became disassociated and began to drift. I wasn't what you would call an athlete, but I was in fairly good shape. I was used to jogging and wandering through the mountains, but the effort required to continue upon this path seemed to multiply with each new bend in the trail. It was as if I was slowly dragging a lifetime of turmoil and regret up the long steep hill. Gasping for breath, I felt like I was drowning.

The heaviness became almost palpable. It was as if something desperately wanted to pull me back into the valley. I began walking for distances of only two hundred steps before stopping to rest. Soon one hundred steps was enough. Something very inhospitable was becoming frightened. It didn't want me to reach the crest. However, this intuitive challenge did nothing but strengthen my resolve. I carefully established my pace, taking my time, going slowly. But I kept going.

Clouds boiled over the peaks from the north and slid down into the high basins. Cold winds began to gust and whine. Flakes of snow intermittently swirled out of the growing fog and turned the rocky ground wet. Everything seemed to be turning gray. I hadn't expected bad weather, but I was prepared. However, I wasn't prepared for the shaking in my legs. I had strayed from what was left of the mining trail and was following a heavily used game trail. Numerous deer and elk tracks covered the ground. Panting, weak and wet with perspiration, I began looking for a place to rest. I was becoming chilled. Occasional breaks in the fog had shown me I was nearing timberline.

Just a few yards ahead was a small grove of gnarled old pines. The trunks were thick and short. The branches were sparse and twisted from blowing wind. I pulled off my soaked sweatshirt and put on a dry wool sweater, then wrapped a waterproof jacket around my shoulders. I hadn't realized how numb my fingers had become. Rubbing them together and blowing warm breath on them, I looked for a place to start a fire. Igniting a wooden match, I carefully presented it to the dry tinder brought along in a plastic bag in my pack. Soon, warm friendly flames greeted my patient hands. I began massaging tired trembling legs.

Dad had always kept a tin or two of kippered herring in his camp box. I had continued the tradition. Placed on a couple of pieces of smashed bread, the fish became a real feast. I finished up with a hot cup of soup and an orange. It was good to just sit quietly upon the mountain. My strength was coming back. Except for my legs, my body felt strong and alive.

The heaviness began to lift. I wanted to go on, but I was concerned about the weather. I decided to rest a while longer and evaluate the situation before proceeding. That wasn't a problem since I didn't really know where I was going or when I had to get there.

Before long, I found myself fondling a prayer feather that I had adorned with gold, crimson and violet ribbons. I tied it on the branch of one of the elder pines that stood before me. There was a short prayer, asking whatever god that there might be to bless my pilgrimage and to keep me safe. I asked the feather to sing the songs that my lips may have forgotten; to help me find the words to the prayers that my heart longed to express.

As it fluttered intermittently in the wind, I found myself watching it with fascination and curiosity. I felt like a cat watching a moving strand of yarn. As is often the case in the mountains, the clouds were soon absorbed back into the crisp thin air and vanished. The sun blazed forth and warmed the chilled earth. I removed my jacket and tied it to the pack. The body was rested. Standing tall and content, I prepared to continue the journey.

I had stopped right at timberline, resting on the shoulder of a ridge that was nestled into a massive spire of granite. The town of Telluride was hidden from view. A gentle puff of wind rustled through the low-lying brush. Then, once again, everything seemed to become quiet. I could almost see into the high green basins. Streaks of orange and red in the outcroppings of rock provided a testimony to the possibility of rich ore. This was a beacon that had brought prospectors here over a hundred years ago in their search for riches. The terrain was becoming much easier. The trail was not so steep. However, after surveying the view, I decided to make my own path across the slide rock and over the saddle of the enticing ridge.

I took my time moving through the unstable rock. It seemed like there were millions of carefully crafted pieces of stone shaped like tear drops. In size they ranged from about twelve to eighteen inches long, maybe a foot wide, but not more than six or eight inches in depth. Strewn carefully over the countryside, they reminded me of scales on the back of a dragon. Remembering the strange heaviness during the first of the journey, I wondered if I had been "tickling the dragon's tail."

I carefully picked my way along the side of the ridge in one long gently rising arc. Sometimes the stones would slip a few inches with the weight of my step. An occasional stumble would produce a brittle rattle that echoed across the gray landscape. Outcroppings of rock were good places to take a break. You could see all the way into Utah, or look down on the miniature trees that had been left far behind. Plodding slowly but incessantly, I eventually reached the edge and peered up and into a previously hidden basin.

To the north, stretching upward like the ramparts of a great castle, was a long curving cliff crowned with crags and exquisitely framed by a crystal blue sky. The slide rock on either side of the basin clung to the mountain as if it were a suspended wave of cascading snow. The granite arms of the citadel reached downward toward the southwest, cuddling an oasis of vibrant life. The grass was radiantly green and thick. There was a small pond fed by a trickle of glacial ice that was hidden beneath the promontory's shadow.

Carpets of green moss and orange-red and silver-gray lichen adorned rocks both large and small. Within moments I was shedding musty socks and plunging tired swollen feet into the refreshing waters. The mirror-like surface reflected a series of shredded clouds crawling over the great granite wall. After placing the second prayer feather on a hardy bush, I munched on a nutritious snack and basked in the triumph of the troublesome climb. Wrapping toes in fresh warm socks, I laced up my boots, stretched out on the ground, and began to rejoice in the ecstasy of pristine wilderness. This was the place that had been calling to me.

Sitting on the other side of the basin was what appeared to be an oval-shaped boulder that was the size of a small house. I wondered how long it had been there. What it would have been like to have seen it come crashing down from the peaks. As I began to stare, it seemed to shimmer and fade and then reappear. Looking more closely, I realized that the shadows of an occasional cloud were probably playing tricks on my vision. A little later, glancing back at the boulder, I noticed that it was actually a small cabin. I marveled at those old-timers, to think of packing timber all that way. I wondered what shape it was in and how it had managed to survive the crushing weight of winter ice and snow.

I listened to the noisy chattering of a little rodent peering from under a rock where she was carefully gathering the bounty of the summer harvest. I wondered how it could survive the harsh winters. While smaller birds searched frantically for seeds and insects, a red-tailed hawk flew into the sun, casting a brief shadow over the rippling pond. The altitude had to be close to thirteen thousand feet. Summer at this elevation lasted just a few weeks. When I looked back at the cabin, I noticed that it had once more turned back into a boulder.

I decided it was time to do some serious investigation. As I gazed across the basin, I thought I caught a glimpse of someone standing near the structure, but I couldn't be sure. It could be a fellow hiker, maybe one of those Rasta folks who sometimes spend time in the mountains. It could even be one of those crazy, extremist rock climbers.

Approaching the site, I discovered an old path. It had become overgrown with bushes and a few wildflowers. Here and there you could see where rocks had been laid out on either side, forming a slightly recognizable border. I began to hear the unmistakable call of a pair of ravens. I was surprised to see them. I didn't realize they were found at this altitude. They squawked and dived around the area and seemed to be taking an interest in my activities. Maybe they were looking for a handout. Maybe I was lost and they were trying to show me the way.

The path led to the base of a little knoll that was maybe fifteen or twenty feet higher than the rest of the terrain. The knoll was a sort of glacial bench stretching out from the walls that formed the alpine basin. It was fairly wide and level. As I climbed up the little ridge, the object of my curiosity came into view. There was an old squareset made of badly weathered timbers, the kind that the old-timers used to place around the entrances to their mines. They were used as a framework to keep rocks and dirt out of the portal or to shore up weak areas deeper inside the tunnel.

It looked like an entrance to an old stone building. The walls were mostly gone, but you could still see a ring of rock forming a circular shape that was approximately twelve to sixteen feet across. In some places the remaining rock was two or three feet high. In some places there were no rocks left. In the center was a small fire, which was being maintained from the remaining scraps of wood that may have come from a roof. I hesitated as I saw a quiet, pathetic-looking figure. He sported a long beard and had an old floor-length coat precariously wrapped around his rounded shoulders. He appeared to be sickly and frail. He reminded me of one of those old miners who was slowly dying from a chronic respiratory illness. He looked up at me with one eye closed and motioned me forward.

As I approached the entryway, one of the ravens swooped down and landed on the top beam of the square set and sat staring at me. Inching forward, a voice coming from the coat reassured me.

"It's all right, I have been watching you. You are welcome here."

As I moved into the circle, I felt a wave of energy and heat. My body began to tingle. All fatigue was gone.

He motioned for me to sit down. A cube-shaped rock that had been placed in front of the fire seemed to suit the purpose. Gazing into the flames, I noticed an old coffee pot. It looked like the one my father had used at the cabin when I was a boy. A feeble, shaking hand attempted to pour the steaming brew into a cup. Some of the liquid splashed into the fire and made a hissing sound.

The cup was handed to me with instructions to drink slowly, taking one sip at a time. When I placed the cup to my lips, it seemed that it was empty. There was no liquid, nothing to taste. Not wanting to offend, I pretended to take a sip.

The old man seemed to change. At first he appeared to be a pathetic version of my father, dying of cancer. Then there was the impression that he might be Oscar. Once I even saw the twinkling eyes of Swamiji looking back at me. With each sip, not only did the man change, but the cup began to change. Each time I put the cup to my lips, the man became stronger and younger. After the first few sips, I noticed that a dark sweet-tasting liquid had begun to appear in the bottom of the cup. Then the old metal cup became an exquisite Grail and disappeared.

Now a middle-aged man was peering out from under a wide-brimmed hat. He told me that since I had accepted his hospitality, I owed him a gift. It was about this time that I realized that our communication had not been in spoken words. The communication was within our own minds. Up to this time the whole process seemed to be a rather casual experience. A wave of apprehension welled up, as it finally began to dawn on my clouded consciousness that something quite remarkable was happening.

I remembered my third and last prayer feather. The prayer feather would be presented with peace, healing, and good will. As a finely manicured hand reached out, the feather burst into light and was absorbed into the old man's coat. An amused but un-nerving grin erupted upon the bearded face as I grabbed at a small Celtic cross that I often wear around my neck.

I wasn't interested in making any pacts with demons. I shud-dered and wondered if I were lost in some sorcerer's cauldron. While struggling to make sense out of it, I realized that I must be asleep and dreaming.

There came a muffled, earthly rumbling sound. It was the purring of a great cat, the jaguar of my vision. Looking down, I re-member seeing a braided leash in my right hand which was made from gold, crimson, and violet strips of leather. I released the guardian. His golden eyes flared with gratitude and devotion. He stretched upward from his seated position and gracefully glided toward the entrance. With each step he took, there appeared an-other large cat, each one a different color. The animals placed themselves around the outside of the circle. The black posi-tioned himself in the north. A tan-colored cougar sat in the east. A white one lounged in the south. A ruddy red one settled in the west. As they began to fall asleep, they faded and disappeared.

As the four-legged ones vanished from the arena, the ravens screamed and fiercely flapped their blue-black wings. The two birds also began to fade, and then two women dressed in ancient battle gear appeared on either side of the entrance. They re-minded me of the lady I had met earlier in the day. They stood as worthy sentinels, guarding a portal that was stretching into another dimension.

Refocusing my attention on my host, I again remembered the prayer feather that had been freely presented in the spirit of peace and friendship. Reading my thoughts, the magician leaped to his feet and spread open his cloak. Inside was possibly every prayer feather I had ever made. A hearty and contagious laugh exploded from deep within his chest. It was the kind of laughter that ends with eyes full of happy tears. I remember making a solemn vow that I would try to recall every detail of what was happening. I was offered an opportunity to end the experience if that was my wish. The process was continued.

His demeanor became more serious. He removed his cloak and turned it inside out. It became a soft leather cape adorned with a multitude of brightly colored feathers and other ornaments. Stern and confident, he commanded that it was time for me to discover the teachings of my ancestors and to reclaim my heritage. He draped the cape around my shoulders. He presented me with a simple walking stick made of aspen. Sometimes it was painted and decorated with feathers and crystals. Sometimes it appeared as a gruesome bloody spear. He may have placed something upon my head, but I don't remember.

Finally, he strapped a cross-hilted sword around my waist. It was one I had seen before, in other dreams. As he grabbed me by the shoulders, his eyes blazed into my soul. He began a prayer in some unknown language. Concluding the initiation, he bade me to always use power wisely.

Everything faded and became dark. I began to see that I was standing in a huge but dimly lit structure. The ceiling was high. It was rectangular in shape, made of massive, handhewn timbers. There was singing and chanting. At this point my mind became dull. It was hard to focus. I began struggling to keep my cycs open, fighting to comprehend the scene before me. It seemed I remained in a stupor for a long period of time. I remember gazing into some writing in some scrolls or books. However, my mind was either unable or unwilling to focus on anything or to comprehend its meaning.

Finally, aroused from my forgetfulness, a soft blue light approached. First it became a sphere, then a planet. It hovered before me. Upon the planet were five pulsating beacons of light placed randomly around the globe. Flowing from these points of light were tiny sparks that meandered across the face of the blue and white orb. As they moved from their points of origin, they became smaller and dimmer. Just before the sparks would go out, they would start returning to their points of origin and become bright once more. Three times the sphere was presented, and three times it began shaking and convulsing and disappeared. The fourth time I reached out and touched it. Scrutinizing the geographical features, I realized this was Planet Earth. I was looking at the North American continent.

Then came more confusion and disorientation. It was as if something was blocking my perception. It was as if my senses could see, but my mind couldn't grasp or recognize what was right before it. Eventually, I found myself back in the seed-shaped ruin upon the mountain. A gnarled old oak had grown where the fire pit had been. A small spring trickled out from under its roots. Two hooded figures, a man and a woman, one dressed in black, one dressed in white; seemed to be picking things off the tree. Acknowledging my presence, they turned and nodded. I knew I should know them, but their identities were hidden from me. I struggled to see what the items were, but to no avail. Each was placing their harvest into a brightly-colored small leather pouch.

In the next scene that I remember, the grand master of this experience had returned. He stood with outstretched arms, holding one pouch in each hand. He explained that in one pouch was thought. In the other pouch was memory. He stuffed them into a larger bag and sprinkled them with sweet smelling herbs. Then he began to gently blow his breath into the entire satchel. When finished, he placed it deep within my backpack, which was now lying at the portal. He told me the meaning of the vision would become clearer as the years wore on; would become clearer as I continued to learn how to remember.

This mysterious guide stood before me: alive, radiant, compassionate, and wise. He wore some kind of tunic covered with a dark blue cloak. The edges of his garments were adorned with

golden strips of braid with blue, red, and green woven in between. His hair and beard were a long ruddy blonde. He wore a
large gold buckle on a wide brown belt. Fur skins tied with strips
of rawhide were wrapped around his legs and ankles. There was a
shining metal medallion around his neck, but I couldn't make
out the details. He wore some kind of headgear that I can no longer remember. As I gazed into his eyes, he reached out his hand
in friendship. We became one. He was gone. I remained, dressed
in his costume.

Looking up at the old oak, I saw the bearded man dressed in a
loin cloth, hanging on the tree. He was in great suffering. The
two hooded attendants, now standing at my side, explained that
this was the grand shaman. The hopes of the world were upon
his shoulders. I began to hear and see multitudes of people
standing in a great circle, singing, praying, and chanting, all
looking toward the tree and the one who was suffering upon it. A
red-cloaked demon appeared brandishing a large jeweled dagger
shaped like a cross. Lunging at the figure upon the tree, he thrust
the dagger deep into his body over and over again. This seemed
to bring great satisfaction to the devilish creature. With one last
breath, the crucified one thanked the demon for allowing him
the honor of the crucifixion and for bringing an end to his torment. With his last bit of strength, he gave his antagonist a
blessing in a language that I didn't recognize. The demon disappeared into a pool of blood that was now flowing from the roots
of the tree. Its leaves turned bright green and it began to grow
rapidly.

The singing, chanting, and praying merged into one loud
harmonious drone. A magnificent red-headed goddess appeared
wearing pagan battle garb. She was accompanied by a dozen or so
ravens who began tearing away strips of quivering flesh from the
already mutilated body. Then, casting her sword into the pool of
blood at the base of the tree, crystal waters gushed forth, cleansing and healing everything in its path as it ran down the
mountain. She became the all-compassionate earth mother
wrapped in shimmering white linen that seemed to glow.

As the comforting drone of chanting voices continued, a gentle golden light began to pulsate. The mangled body transformed into a radiant beam of light, reaching from deep into the earth and up into the heavens. A huge spotted eagle emerged from the beacon and screamed triumphantly. Its powerful voice echoed, then thundered through the mountains. I watched the spirit eagle climb steadily upward in ever-widening spirals until it was out of sight.

The last thing I remember was being escorted by the two warrior maidens. They were taking me back through the portal. As I struggled to retain what I had experienced, they told me not to be concerned, that they would help me remember what I needed to know when the time was right.

Something was pressing against my back. It was hard and uncomfortable, a pointed rock. I sat up. I had been laying on the side of the hill, my pack placed under my head. Around me was a beautiful array of wildflowers. From this one vantage point I could see Ingram Falls, Bridal Veil Falls, and the Bear Creek Falls. I was no longer within the basin. I don't know how long I had slept there or how I had gotten back down to the foothills. I finished the last few gulps of water. The last prayer feather was gone. Close by was a winding trail that led back down to Tomboy Road. It was as if time had collapsed. It seemed like it only took a few minutes to return to the Jeep.

How to explain, how to express the events of that day. Although everything looked familiar, it was as if I had been gone for a thousand years. I was very, very weary, but peaceful and content. After a small dinner, I went to bed as memories and images of the experience flickered through my consciousness like the playful flames of what I came to realize was Wodan's fire.

Since then, I have scoured the horizon and studied the maps. However, I still have no idea of where I had been. Nothing looks quite like that enchanted basin that was discovered as I wandered out of the fog and over the ridge. It is difficult to know when the dream started and when it ended. From the tattered remnants of my memory I have pieced together all that I can recall.

At the moment I awoke on the hillside, I was perfectly willing to admit that I was thoroughly insane. However, the events of that day were so intriguing and expansive in their implications that I knew I would be following this path to its conclusion, no matter where it would lead. I had come too far to turn back.

Chapter Fourteen

Revelation Upon the Mountain

Being slowly and methodically orchestrated by some grand and omnipotent force, the subtle but definite dawning continued. With direction and guidance from the Source and a growing intimacy with the cyclic moods of the earth comes an evolving realization. There has come a recognition that we had been brought to the mountain to rediscover the essential nature and purpose of the sacred promontory.

The words that follow may be for contemplation or discussion. However, the contemplation or discussion is not for deciding if the words are right or if they are wrong. For these words are not opinions, they are teachings. Teachings just are. And they are always true, whether we understand them or not. At times, teachings have a way of seeming simplistic, archaic, or obscure. Sometimes it is difficult to fully appreciate their implications. They often require a period of time for observation and reflection before the wisdom embodied within them can be brought into an arena where they can be harvested and offered up for the nourishment of famished souls.

Allow me to continue the story, to share with you a true story of humankind's sojourn within this earth. For now it is given that during this time the primal teachings of a sacred mountain may be remembered, resurrected, and reclaimed.

Through the ages, souls have sought to discover the ancient location of what has been called the Garden of Eden. Some say it is here. Some say it is there. Some claim that it is only a mythical, symbolic metaphor for the birthplace of the human race. The multitudes seldom think about it or even consider such a thing to be a relevant issue. Yet, others have spent lifetimes searching for their Brigadoon, Shangri-la, or El Dorado.

In a time just after the great heavenly battles subsided, in a time that was not yet a time and in a place that was not yet a place, it was ordained by the Creator that the spirit that was becoming human would merge into the planet and take upon itself bodies of flesh that were suited to the environment that was already under their exploration. The nature of these original beings is too ancient and complex for the present conscious mind to comprehend. However, it can be said that the number of this developing human beingness became five. We bear evidence of this through the manifestation of our physical bodies. We have five appendages emerging from the trunks of our bodies: two arms, two legs, and a head. We come with five digits on each hand and foot. We are endowed with five earthly senses: seeing, hearing, touching, smelling, and tasting.

As we reached out of the spirit world and plunged deeply into human beingness, we sprang forth from not one, but from five separate locations. There were five cradles of divine spirit where that-which-was-to-become-human was wrapped in physical bodies of their own. We would no longer be required to seize and inhabit the bodies and spirits of the animals and meddle with the nature of the elements of the earth in order to participate in the earthly kingdom. As conscious soul evolved into conscious mind, we plunged deeper and deeper into numbing material denseness and began to lose strength, purpose, and knowledge. Soon, many things could only be understood through the archetypical myths and symbolism that call to us from out of the mysteries of the unconscious domain.

These five places are not mythological places. They are real places, but they are the places where all myth began. These five centers are also the primary chakra centers of the planet. They breathe the breath of life into Earth Mother and help moderate the cyclical cataclysms that befall our world in ways that a few scientists are just beginning to suspect. Each of these five points is made up of several smaller points that form the unity and power that is embodied within each region. Within these sacred citadels great powers and forces continue to wage the ancient and primal battles between the forces of good and evil, beauty and debauchery, peace and turmoil. Through this duality of opposites there is the generation of the tension that induces the ever-evolving process of creation and the promotion of the continual natural cycles necessary for the existence of a living planet. This is the place where the breath of life is breathed into our nostrils and we become souls that are alive within the earth.

Each center tends to have its own purpose and personality. These are the places where angels congregate and the great masters dwell. These are the places where the archetypes for the great hosts of spirit beings were first conceptualized and brought into manifestation. Sometimes when the conditions are right, pilgrims come to these places and have bursts of seeing, remembering, and understanding.

These chakra centers are living beacons radiating within the planet that eternally show us the way home, the way back to the stars and beyond. They are rallying points of grace and divine intervention. Just visiting such a place can induce a state of bliss in those who are able to heed the call and recognize their sanctity. Once one is truly able to recognize the presence within these holy steads, it is possible for sacredness to be recognized and acknowledged in a thousand places and in a thousand different ways.

These are places of tremendous beauty and power. They are places where the soul can have the opportunity to reaffirm itself and remember its origin and purpose. They are places where great teachings are born, crucified, and resurrected. For sure, there are other places of great power and beauty, but these five are the primal, ancestral birthplaces of the people that live within this planet.

One center is located in the south of the African continent in a country called Zimbabwe. Another is located high in the Himalayas on the Asian continent near and around Mount Meru. A third is located under the Pacific Ocean near the South Sea

Islands. A fourth is located high in the Andes of Peru near Machu Pichu. The last is located within and around the sacred valley that is now called Telluride. The Source has suggested that this sacred center may be referred to as the Adnipoche.

At the time of the beginning, it was ordained that, in addition to there being five centers upon the planet, there would be five ages in which the human beings would be allowed to live and grow and inhabit the planet. At the conclusion of each age, the surface would be scoured clean just before the beginning of each succeeding age or epoch. The cycles would come just like the changing of the seasons: a time of culmination and decay, then a resting and rejuvenation before another period of rebirthing and flourishing.

At this time we are poised upon the last moments of the fourth world, a world that has lasted tens of thousands of years. The transition may be harsh or gentle, but there will be a transition before the coming of the fifth and final age. It may come quickly as a great devastation or slowly over several generations, but it will come. The choice is forever in our hands. It is for us to choose. Our actions are already deciding whether or not it will come in waves of anguish and torment, or waves of healing and joy.

In addition to the five centers and the five times, it was ordained at the time of the beginning that there would be five races. The original races were black, blue, red, white, and yellow. At this time there are no longer any pure races. As time continues, it may be possible that the many races will become one. But this is not yet certain. Each of the five centers is to be equally celebrated and treasured by all five races, for all five centers and all five races are manifestations of the same one Creator. Although some return over and over again within the same race, it should always be remembered that most souls live their many lives within the several races and the many cultures that have blossomed during our earthly sojourn.

Toward the end of each age there is an explosion of population and migration. Within the genes and the blood of the flesh bodies, there sometimes begins an intense restlessness that is similar to the urging the salmon feels as it returns to its spawning grounds. However, never has there been seen such a massive shifting and growth of the populations until this current age. Never have the resources of this living planet been taxed so heavily by those that are called the human beings. The first age may be referred to as the Adz. The second age may be referred to as the Lemurian Age. The third age has sometimes been called the Atlantean Age. The fourth age is not yet named. The fifth is soon to come.

It is also given that during the culmination and the beginning of the transition into each age, one race or culture tends to dominate the planet and the other races. The quality of stewardship and wisdom demonstrated in that time by that race will be a direct reflection of the severity of the calamities that will befall the planet as it moves into the next cyclical transition.

One transition was so volatile and devastating that the blue race has been almost entirely obliterated and absorbed into the remaining peoples of the earth. One can still see a slight tinge of blue in the blackness of some of the African and Australian peoples. It is through the sacrifice and grace of that ancient race that the opportunities of these and other times have continued. The sacred center of that race, lying beneath the ocean, surrounded by the ring of fire, still moans, creaks, and rattles, bearing witness to the cataclysm of destructive ways. The blue race now serves as the point of integration, located at the center of the circle of life. The symbolism of the circle often represents the unity of the one God and can depict the four directions, the four seasons, and the four remaining races.

Periodically, through the generations, these five primal earth chakras and their numerous younger brothers and sisters call out to the people to return to the ancient teachings and the ancient ways. They call out for the people to remember their origin, to grow in wisdom and harmony, and to fulfill their destiny. It is the earth's most ancient and halcyon cry pouring forth both its blessing and its warning that another judging and harvesting is growing ever so near. For it is given that there shall be five opportunities for the soul to enter or leave this hardened realm; five opportunities to return with power and grace to the Great Being from whence we came; five opportunities to complete the mission, to merge with the illumined ones, and to return as stars in the crown of our Creator.

This was the essential teaching that was remembered through the pilgrimage upon the mountain. This was my soul's birthplace into this earthly realm. It is the place through which I can still reach out and discover the loving arms of my Creator, revive my soul, and become empowered by the other worlds and dimensions of power and wisdom.

And now we are here. We have come to an end of a remembering of the ancient archetype upon which our ancestral migrations are founded. We are here, creating the latest Chapter of our experience within the earth. We find ourselves propelled into a harried culture, generating massive systems of information and technology. However, knowledge and wisdom struggle to keep pace and too often lag behind.

The white race returns to its "New World" with a horrible hunger. It comes stumbling blindly back toward the primal garden with a terrible affliction. It has forgotten its roots. We have forgotten who we are, where we come from, and where we are going. We have forgotten that we too were once an aboriginal and indigenous people. We know little or nothing of our pagan past and heritage. We have forgotten the ways of our ancestors. The white tribes scamper around the planet afflicted with modern, new age religions and dogmas replete with teachings that have too often become twisted and driven by narcissistic and selfish ends. Too many of us come with a mindset burdened by consumption, conquest, and domination.

I have spent much of this life watching and partaking of an evolving struggle for spiritual rebirth. We have often sought the sacred power within the dancing void by ravenously devouring the traditions of others. Often feeling unfulfilled by the explanations of the religions of this age, many have sought the

glimmerings of light radiating through the Native American shaman and the Eastern teachers. We have struggled to rediscover
and to become a part of something ancient and sacred. We struggle to recapture ways of seeing and knowing that don't end at
sundown.

Although fascinating and empowering, too often there is still
something missing. It is as if we are dressing up in someone else's
clothing because it feels much better than what we are usually
wearing. But no matter how much better we may feel, the stark
truth is that we are too often borrowing and absorbing traditions
that are not our own. They do not belong to us. It would appear
that we come in what might be called a Judeo-Christian wrapper.
However, it is becoming clear to many that something has been
left out. And no matter how comforting and familiar the trappings
of our churches appear to be, many of us are left with a sense that
our spiritual and cultural heritage is lacking or incomplete.

Further is the confusion made when one realizes that many
of us who now live in this modern world once lived in other
times and celebrated pagan traditions as the shaman and yogis of
other races and cultures. Not finding any familiar philosophical
niche or lifestyle in this time, we too often become isolated and
alienated, while a subtle but relentless gnawing weighs heavily
upon our soul.

We may find ourselves humbled by the beauty and power of
wilderness. But whether we stand in awe of it or see it as something to be conquered and to be beaten into submission, it is a
rare "Caucasian" who has a clear sense of our interconnectedness to living, breathing earth. Few of us are still able to
remember or to recognize the presence of the Creator in the creation. There are fewer still who have a mythology and a
ceremony in which to express it. To feel comfortable in wilderness and to know how to participate harmoniously within the
circle of life with passionate ceremony has become a muffled
memory rather than an inalienable birthright.

Still, we watch and absorb the pagan ceremonies of other cultures. We buy the art that reflects a closeness and knowledge of

earth, sky, air, and water in recognition of our souls' longing for a reconnection with sacred things. We ravenously devour the books and mythology that have a familiar ring and soothe the silent emptiness that comes from deep within the heart and soul.

When we come to the aboriginal circle of the other pagan races and cultures, we bring no creation stories, no sacred drums, talismans, or fetishes, for firsthand knowledge of these things has been suppressed and hidden from our consciousness. Yet here we stand, feeling inspired and mesmerized by the power and bliss of sacred objects and intimate ceremony.

All too often, the only response we know is to become as ignorant and helpless imitators of the traditions of others and to lay our consciousness on the altar of shame, anger, or confusion. For some, the shame is a symptom of a sickness born of the multitude of atrocities that white tribes have perpetrated toward their pagan brothers and sisters during this modern time of conquest and domination.

As we fan the conviction that our lifestyle must prevail at all costs, we generally ignore the effect that our twisted ideology is having on others. Even as we struggle to become conscious and cast off the delusion, we still insatiably wage a not-so-subtle war of perspective and economics that requires that we either grind all others into like-minded submission or destroy them. The concept of tolerance or coexistence is totally unacceptable to a dogma that can comprehend no other point of view than its own.

It is not easily seen or understood that this hurtful way of being is an affliction and a disease. It is not the way the race is. It is not the way that it is meant to be. All the races of the earth have been or shall become afflicted from time to time with this same elixir of forgetfulness, disconnectedness, and perversity. It is always easier to see the bearer of illness as being the illness itself, rather than one who is simply overcome by the disease.

If these words seem harsh, this is good. They are doing their job. They are meant to be harsh. For we have been harsh. We continue to be harsh. And this truth must be faced objectively and truthfully, even as we recognize that there has also been extraordinary learning, healing, and goodness. Many continue to be driven from somewhere deep within where their instincts for spiritual survival are alive and howling. We are driven onward toward our halcyon quest. The innate drive to continue our search into the American wilderness has served us well.

But meanwhile, it is important to remain brutally aware that there continues to be the burgeoning forth of much folly, ignorance, and selfishness. The hidden disease is festering. It will no longer be possible to keep it hidden. It is about to reveal itself. Each will come to this realization in their own time, place, and way. It is festering now, within the earth, within our communities, within our families and our individual psyches. This is a disease that knows no race or religion, but uses them both for its divisive and destructive ends. This age is dangerously courting a time when "the enemy way" may become the supreme paradigm that ensnares all of creation.

It is too easy to imprison one's gods behind a finely credentialed façade of masonry, clergy and protocol. We find it useful to continuously reselect, rewrite, and reinterpret the scripture that allows us to become more and more distant from the truth of our pagan roots. The modern quest has been to submit, believe, and serve; to become saved, sanctified, and enlightened in one final, eternal, and dramatic moment. We ignore the eternal wisdom of the Creator made manifest through the voice of the perennial cycles of pristine wilderness.

We are too often duped into believing that in one infantile act we can complete our egocentric obligation to our soul and then return to the usual superficial dullness and gluttony of our high-tech addictions. Yes, we have become as little children placing our faith in the magic and mystery of a fairy tale Santa Claus. We have become enraptured in the hypermania of his wonder and joy. But too often we are not willing to grow up and to see the warning of the trolls and the toil of the creator's elves, sprites, and angels that make it all possible. Too often we are not willing to clean up the mess once the toys have been left unwrapped, broken, and scattered beneath the sacrificial tree.

Much of this was done in the name of an evolving mythos of a risen Christ that rose from the ashes of the Roman Empire. They came with an arrogant and ravenous conviction that they were the only ones capable of correctly divining spiritual truth. That truth, or way of seeing, by its very nature dictated that all must be converted or conquered and consumed to the glory of their god.

This was a god that backed Europe's lust for gold, land, and slaves. This new state religion claimed to believe in one god. However, in truth, it was a polytheistic orientation. It believed in at least two gods: a god that was good called Jesus who had a heavenly father and an earthly mother; and a god who was evil called Satan, as well as a legion of angels, seraphim, and cherubim.

The way to alleged salvation became riddled with the corpses of conquered empires and shattered traditions. He was correct in warning that many would come in His name saying He was the Christ, but they would be false prophets and should not be followed or listened to. He said He came with a sword, but He also comes to fulfill, and recreate not to destroy. He said that greater love has no man than to put down his life for his brother. Somehow that message became twisted and reversed. It is clear that we need not wait for the arrival of the Anti-Christ. He is already with us. He is alive and well and thrives right within our midst.

It would seem that first this Messiah was crucified. Then His teachings were crucified. The teachings have yet to become fully resurrected. Is it any wonder that this Prince of Peace said He would need to return. It would appear that there are still more Chapters to be written.

This is not a phenomenon whose roots flourish solely within Christendom. Let us look also at what has become of the other religions that have been developed during the later part of this fourth age. There too lie houses divided and engaged in battles designed to once and for all dominate and destroy both the gentile and the infidel. Each of the many sides is struggling to demonstrate for all time the supremacy of the one true doctrine. These stand poised to begin the war of wars. They seem to have learned little from the teachings of their prophets.

Fear-based religions and dogma do not last. They are eventually eaten up by their own hatred and egocentric arrogance. Harmony is the result of love put into action. True redemption does not require an enemy to give it purpose and to justify its actions. Perfect love casts out all fear.

All this should not be seen as merely a battle of gods and religions. It is a part of the various aspects of the human soul that constantly recycles and has its season. It is time to see it for what it is. It is the eternal battle that allows us to experience, to learn, and to grow. It might even be said that the evil is not our enemy, but it is our friend and teacher. It allows us to be challenged, to grow, to become strong and insightful. When we run from the demon, we are devoured by our own fear and faithlessness. When the fears are bravely faced and understood, we are made strong and whole. When devils are conquered, there is no need for messiahs. When messiahs are conquered, there is no need for devils. Today's god often becomes tomorrow's Satan.

When the true messiah comes or when that messianic force is invoked, it is not Indian, Hindu, Islamic, Buddhist, Christian, or pagan. No matter what name it may be given, it is purely and simply the anointed messianic force. It belongs to no one people, place, or tradition. It manifests as it will, in a thousand places, in a thousand ways. It comforts. It heals. It resurrects. It combines. It challenges and inspires. It makes things whole again. It does not condemn, dominate, destroy, conquer, and devour. Those things are a manifestation of something else, something that is not loving, forgiving, and full of life.

If one looks closely enough, there can be seen new life emerging through the cracks of shifting and collapsing foundations. Before this current age of the enemy way, there was an old age of perennial wisdom that has not gone away. It was merely resting. It has been resting because this is the nature of things; this is the way things are. It is a part of the continuing circle of cycles.

This wisdom is not the formation of a new age. It is merely another emerging episode within a series of ancient ages. The re-emergence of ages when sacred scriptures are not read, but written. An age when prophets, angels, and messengers are not statues in temples that are remembered in interesting stories, but an age when they are greeted and talked to as we journey together along the path. Kill them if you must, but they shall always return.

We too had holy men and sacred women who could span the shackles of time and space and bring us word of other ways of being and knowing. We even had a god who hung from a tree in order to bring sacred knowledge and blessings back to his people. We too had strong ties to the natural world and the elemental kingdoms. We too knew of the healing spirits that dwell within sacred plants that could be coaxed into service. We too have worn the feathers of the great spotted eagle, a symbol of the Allfather who leads our wolf-warriors into great spiritual battles. We too have known sacred groves and living rocks and healing waters. We too have wandered across the wilderness for many centuries, lived in harmony within the earthly domain, and found favor in the great Mother and her countless goddesses.

It is time to remember that the Norse folk believed in an afterlife and an end of the world called Ragnarok (Armageddon), long before the progression of Italian popes. It is time to remember that the protective amulets of Thor's hammer hung around the necks of true believers while evolving Christianity was still identified by the symbol of the fish. It should be remembered that our ancestors wore the crossed sun-wheel of Wodan, the Allfather, long before we converted to Middle Eastern crosses.

Somehow, within a few short centuries, a messiah who taught love, peace, and forgiveness became the focal point of a politicized dogma that resulted in the destruction and genocide of a hundred cultures and millions of people around the planet. It has been forgotten that hordes of Christian warlords massacred, slaughtered and then absorbed the remaining Teutonic and Scandinavian tribes. They maimed, tortured, and butchered our sanctified pagan priests and priestesses. They defiled and desecrated our holy sanctuaries centuries before they finally became aware of a New World in the West. Usurping the power of the trusting and the faithful, the demon has grown fat on fruit that it has not earned.

The momentum of the movement spread across the oceans where canonized conquistadors enslaved and slaughtered tens of thousands and then millions of the so-called Indians. This new age culture spread and mutated across the face of what it termed its New World, invading the western hemisphere from pole to pole.

We want to be forever young, never in pain, and always in bliss. While we debase and ignore the wisdom of cyclical creation, we wrap ourselves in magical cults of positive thinking and live in a world of denial. In truth, we are as Merlin, the shaman, who lives backwards. Foregoing all we have learned, we are blustering through our terrible twos and about to be absorbed back into the womb of the Creator's primal wisdom.

Most of us are totally unaware of a sixteen-hundred-year process of erosion and suppression of the spiritual heritage of an entire race of people. We have been seduced into ways of thinking and ways of being that are alien to our ancestral nature. We have lost our heritage and have replaced it with a recent new age conglomerate of Middle Eastern traditions. We have allowed asphalt and concrete to block out the joy and pride of our own pagan roots. All too often this disease that we have suffered during this period of isolation and ignorance journeys with us and spreads its chaos of conquest and possessiveness across the face of the planet.

The memories of sacred ground have been ripped from our consciousness. Yet we travel throughout our nation on pilgrimages called vacations, where we stand in awe of the power of the remaining areas of pristine wilderness. We stand mesmerized as we visit the pueblos and feel the power of sacred rattling and drumming, not knowing that we too used to summon the holy presence and ask it to bless our clans and heal our lands and let our people live.

Mainstream America does not know that their European ancestors once danced and chanted around sacred fires beneath pagan moons. We have forgotten that our own clans once created pottery out of rich moist earth, adorned with symbols of power and life. We have forgotten our own myths and stories about tricksters and shapeshifters. We mutilate and copy the sacred inipi ceremony, but remain unaware that the people in Scandia and throughout the world have also used "sweat lodges" as sacred places of purification, ceremony, and healing.

We have forgotten the wisdom of the great circle of life with all its seasons and ceremonies. And yet, right under our noses, the eggs, bunnies, sacred boughs of holly, and mistletoe linger. And "Christmas trees," yule logs, and sacred evergreen wreaths continue to fascinate us.

It has only been during this recent new age that we have come to believe that the one true God could only speak out of one book, from one culture, at one time, and in one place. Many new age Christians have failed to realize that sorcery and witchcraft in the name of Jesus is still just sorcery and witchcraft. And love and healing in the name of pagan wisdom is still love and healing by whatever name you wish to call it.

It is time for my people to remember who they are and where they come from. It is time to recognize that we too are a displaced and indigenous people. We too have a rich pagan heritage and have had knowledge of sacred earth. It is hard for us to remember. It is hard because we were among the first to fall during this modern era.

There were few anthropologists and photographers in those times. Up into this last century it was still possible to find some remnants of the pagan cultures in northwest Europe. Scandia was the last old world pagan stronghold that fell to the god of the New Age. When it did fall, the onslaught continued across the oceans of the world.

Now is the time of remembering. Now is the time to reclaim our roots, complete our wanderings and return to our own place within the natural order of things. Now is the time to embrace the wisdom of the past and the great discoveries unfolding within our future. The circle of our great pilgrimage from the primal centers will not be completed until we can bring back our own ancestral knowledge, sacred ways, and ceremonies. When we come to the circle with knowing and remembering of our own traditions, then we will be full. When we return with fierce loyalty as equal members of the ever-flowing circle of the one Creator, then there shall come healing and harmony and the next rendition of the cultural vessels that display the eternal truths will once again begin to manifest.

The old ways recognized that things are periodically interrupted by natural cycles of restful death and decay before a new time of rebirth and growth. We have grown old and forgetful. We have forgotten the cold silent winters that melt into blossoming springs and grow into ripened summers that fade with a flurry of color and bountiful harvesting. These ages come and go like waves on the seashore—waves that don't ask why, waves that relentlessly seek to reclaim the harmonic balance, waves that reflect an agitated sea that stretches far past our limited horizons.

The evil one would hide from you the truth that all things have their time, purpose and season. That which is truly evil would have you believe that one side must win and one side must lose. This is the great lie that the demon beast always seeks to impart. The great deceiver would have you believe that there must be a battle and that the battle is to destroy evil. The great dragon beast struggles and fights to maintain our conviction that this is so.

We need to recover our wisdom and knowledge of the duality, walk the razor's edge, and rediscover the beauty way. We need to realize that we do not have to choose up sides and eternally do battle. We can also decide to pick both sides or to pick no side. We can choose, and we do choose every day. It is the evil one's task to limit the choices and to make us think that the choices it offers are somehow the only ones available. It camouflages the true teachings that would reveal the relentless clandestine seduction of the enemy way. It seeks to disturb the balance and to induce the strife. It is the path that leads to disharmony, disease, and death. It is that which seeks to deny the wisdom of the great circle of life.

However, the Creator is not mocked. All is in order. This eternal pattern is the primal core of a healthy universe. Yes, we have forgotten, but many are beginning to remember. The same Great Being that creates the one God also creates the many gods, and each has a place and season. We need to know ourselves and recognize our gods in all seasons, times, and places. Then we can stand firm in the ever-flowing knowledge of pristine spirit, and no heaven or hell will ever seduce us again.

Because a resurrection is near, a crucifixion has begun. An ancient priest clan is stirring, preparing for rebirth, beginning its rise through the falling ashes. It cannot be stopped any more than one can stop the grass that awakens in the spring or snow that returns in winter. It is the phoenix rising from its own ashes.

The wizened dragon beast shudders within its calloused cavern of panic and fear, tormented by all that it has done and all that it has not done. For those who pray and those who meditate, for those who heed the call, there is nothing to fear except the melting walls of our own dungeons of imprisoning delusion.

Chapter Fifteen

Answered

The sulfur-tipped match pops and sizzles as it flares and bursts into flame. The sting of burning sulfer awakens dulled senses. Resting next to the wick, the small white candle slowly absorbs the flickering orange tongue and begins to glow. The light of the one candle fills the darkened room.

Stirred by a dream, I rose before the dawn and went to the sadhana room. There, within the stillness, the contemplation continued. The litany of extrasensory stimulation was beginning to unravel. A relentless emptiness had erupted, demanding to know what was the point of all these visionary experiences, dreams, and profusions of channeled information. Somewhere in the drama of sacred pilgrimage and shamanic visions, purpose and meaning had become overshadowed. Although scintillating and fascinating, it seemed that at best there had begun a recollection of ancient soul memories and a discovery of other levels of existence with which one might interact. However, it all seemed to be just another rendition of familiar and monotonous characters all clamoring to begin yet another act of the same worn-out, never-ending plot. This was the fourth age. A fifth is expected.

All that had essentially been discovered is that the same archetypal battles with the same primal issues rage on and on regardless of any particular age or place. It seems that sometimes we just play the game better than we do at other times. Sometimes we win a little. Sometimes we lose a little. Meanwhile, time and space just keep on flowing. All of the same eternal forces were continually at work; whether one was battling against or for these opposing forces of duality seemed to be of little consequence. The battles just keep raging on and on and on.

The characters could be found right in the midst of a real estate office just as well as within some esoteric astral realm. So what's all the fuss about? What's the point in continuing to widen the game plan to ever-expanding arenas of engagement? I was growing weary of the onslaught of ideas and experiences. It was time to cast off the maze of teachings, ideas, and pseudo-accomplishments. Time to get simple, to reclaim the essence of what makes life worthwhile.

I wasn't really sure of how to do that. Perhaps the Source could be seduced into an inspiring reading that would bring it all back together. Perhaps a trip to Swamiji was the way. It is strange how this whole turn of events erupted after consultation and initiation with Guru Dev. However, this was a time to reach out on my own. It was a time to dredge up the essence of the questing and to at last make the attempt to look deep into the stuff of which the soul is made. It was time to put the parlor games behind me and face whatever essential truth might be claimed.

The mood was rich and dramatic. The clearer I began to see the issue, the more natural and unshakable the resolve became. It was as if I could not live another day without attending to this most important of all issues. It was as if somewhere there had been set an unalterable appointment, and the time was now. Somewhere in the universal chronology of things I was being told, "Yes." Now is the time. This is the place. The time and place to discover what the hungry soul has been seeking. The time to reaffirm the ancient commitment and to reclaim the ancient knowing.

I went to my closet and selected three treasured objects that represented the decades of questing and searching. Something from the Judeo-Christian heritage, something from the experiences with Native American culture, and something from the Eastern traditions.

Charging upward toward the heart of the sacred promontory, the Jeep rattled and shook and began to lose power in the thin alpine air. High in the slide rock, running out of road, I left the vehicle and continued on foot. I pushed onward and upward into

that sacred vortex, that acknowledged gateway to the source of
this soul's creation.

The winds howled around a large flat rock that was warmed by
the rising sun. Upon this pagan altar was placed the Bible given to
me by my mother when I was eight years old. A steel sevachra
(bracelet) inscribed with the mantra Guru Dev had imparted to
me was placed in the east. The jaguar fetish, as seen in my vision,
was placed in the west. I sat in the south and chanted and prayed.
After a while I gathered up the sacred objects and casually tossed
them into a cleft by the rock. It was time to be still. It was time to
put aside all but the essential gnawing. I stretched out on the hard
uneven surface of the rock. I felt filled with the power of conviction. Then I felt very small, fragile and humble.

A passing cloud blocked the sun's rays and threatened rain.
For a few moments the body felt cold and weak. It was good to
feel the return of the warm rays of the sun. Basking upon the
rock, I realized I had brought no food, water, or warm clothing.
But, it didn't matter. I began to relax, listening to my pulse and
breath. I began to reflect on how emotional and willful I had become. Certainly, this was not the way. Swamiji would remind me
that what I was seeking was already here. He would probably ad-
vise that I merely needed to cast off the delusion of all the mind's
meaningless churning. I began to feel foolish, remembering the
immature attempt to call God's promises down out of the sky
while sitting upon another rock one Sunday long ago. Still, I lingered upon the rock. The gnawing that had called me to the rock
was as yet unanswered. It was still calling.

It seemed that nothing had changed. For all my alleged
knowledge and dreaming, I was once more back to a pilgrimage
into the wilderness hoping against hope to somehow pull all of
these experiences together and put them into some kind of
meaningful perspective. I began to acknowledge a growing feeling that I would not move from this place until I was answered.
However, I was not sure if that was my decision or the decision of
this force that was relentlessly taunting me. I just knew that I
had to be there at that time, at that place, on that day.

As time passed, I realized I had not told anyone where I was going. I realized that my wife might become concerned if it took some time before return. However, such matters didn't seem important. I decided to trust that the Source would provide any information that she might need. The Source. That was strange. How is it that one could have access to this interesting phenomena that represents itself to be the source of all knowledge and experience, yet by its own admonition it dictates that one must find one's peace within the confines of one's own consciousness. I was already familiar with that bit of information, but I was never quite sure what to do with it. As time passed I wasn't sure what I was supposed to be doing. I wasn't praying, chanting, or meditating. I began once more to doubt the rationality of this aching quest. Still, I lingered upon the rock.

It seemed that there was no place to go and nothing to do. It seemed infantile to attempt to will your way into communion with the infinite. However, I wasn't really doing that. I was just slowly imploding within the weariness of the search. This recurrent and sometimes insistent sense of longing seemed to take on various shapes at different times.

Yet, when all is quiet and I am blatantly honest with myself, there is always that subtle something that calls out, that something that seems to say you have some unattended business. You have a mission to fulfill. It was as if I had been commissioned to put together some familiar puzzle, but I had never been given all the pieces.

My life wasn't all that bad. According to most perspectives, I was fairly successful. Just being able to have a home in Telluride was quite an accomplishment. I was content with my marriage, proud of my children. Reviewing my psychological training and profile, I mused that I was probably just missing some developmental stage of my childhood, or suffering from some unresolved trauma that induced a post-traumatic stress disorder. Perhaps I was just "burned out" with an interesting set of colorful hallucinations. In Telluride, of course, you can blame everything on the altitude.

The essence of it all was that it was time to put it into some kind of lasting perspective, to somehow come to some conclusion regarding the purpose and meaning of it all. That was why I was here; not to bless or condemn, not to propose or to dispose, but perhaps just to be. I wondered how long I would stay upon the rock. At times, waves of restless energy pulsated through my unraveling mind. Still, I lingered.

It was as if I could choose to think and wonder about these things, or I could choose to be silent. But whichever approach was decided, I knew I would remain here on the rock. I was waiting for something. For what, I really did not know. At some point I don't even think I cared. Eventually, the fidgeting mind, weary of its machinations, just stopped, relaxed, and watched.

After a time, I began to feel some subtle tingling throughout the body. I began to experience what some call the astral or spirit body. It was like a force field that existed within my physical body. This had been experienced several times before, several times during childhood and college years, and a few times while practicing arcane yoga kriyas. I remember how it had come just before the encounter with the jaguar that lives within the natural earth kiva. It began to twist and stretch and then rock back and forth, as if a hidden part of me was coming to life.

It was at least unusual, if not altogether odd, that I didn't feel particularly concerned or reactive to this otherwise disorienting activity. Relaxing into a deeper communion with this inner phenomena, I noticed that, although my eyes were open, I didn't seem to be seeing anything. Soon the activity began to intensify. I could feel myself tumbling and swirling, stretching and shrinking. Consciousness became focused in all directions all at once. After what I perceived to be a short nap, I found myself hovering above the quiet motionless body. Then it was as if I was in all times at all places. And with the slightest prompting, attention could be honed to a single infinitesimal point of passive concentration. As I observed these experiences, the mind began to flutter. It would realize that it had stopped thinking and would briefly revive the chatter, and then disappear into the stillness once again.

I became aware of stretching deeply into the mountain. It was as if the promontory had become my body. I became acutely aware of every level of its existence. I could feel the gentle dripping, trickling, and gushing of a thousand infant rivers and streams. I could commune with the hundreds of miles of tunnels, miners and geologists probing and exploring the hidden depths of the pristine garden of minerals. I could sense the quiet, inquisitive minds of excited yet baffled physicists struggling to unlock and to harness the secret of the promontory's power. I could feel both the strength and the anguish of the mountain as well as its incredible knowing and compassion. It was as if I could feel and flow with the breath of constant undaunted creation. At that moment, I and the land were one.

Then a myriad of images of times, places, people, and spirit beings began to emerge from an unknown source. They flowed toward, around, and past my point of consciousness. They became rapid and blurred. It was no longer possible to comprehend them. I was no longer sure where I was or what was happening. I realized I could resist the process, but I didn't want to. I recall taking one long deep breath and thinking that I would once again trust whatever God there might be to safely guide my way.

I was thrust into a vast expansive world. The primitive world of sight, sound, texture, taste, and smell was revealed as a poorly reflected shadow that began to lose its relevance. I was as a struggling infant captured within a sea of unintelligible sensations, delightfully puzzled and amused, attempting to discover some order in the unraveled tapestry of time and space. The mind continued to relax and disassemble. It seemed somehow widened. It became more of an aperture than something that actively processes, evaluates, and creates.

Then came a magnificent emerging. The soul was enlivened and awakened. I could feel the joy and power of the Creator breathing within and around me. Adesh was answered. It was a thing that now I can only playfully attempt to describe through the mystery of metaphor.

It is as if every question is answered at the precise moment that the wondering begins, so there is never need for doubting or questing. Every feeling of need or desire is precisely fulfilled just before it is sought. There is nothing to do or to be. There is no need to be filled. There is only the recognition and the acknowledgment of the all-pervading presence of the graceful redemption.

The holy presence, so familiar, so personal that it defies need for discussion or description. So pristine, so pure in its simplicity that once it has been touched, it becomes obvious that it has always been right here with us and between us, within the very fabric of our being. It is cleverly hidden within the midst of all creation, enshrouded by the guilt, shame, and fear of our self-imposed limitations. I experienced how we have become our own betrayers. Though we live a blinded muted life, the presence never fades and never leaves us. Everywhere does it manifest. It is the everywhere and the everything. If we are here, it is here. It is such a familiar and comfortable place. I have been here many times, and many times I have forgotten. But for now I was once more alive.

I feel a gentle shudder and become aware that if I remain in this place much longer, it will not be possible to return. Becoming more and more self-conscious, I feel the familiar cavern calling me back. Though enlightened and enlivened, it would appear that, if there is an illumination, that time is not yet at hand.

The great resistance, fueled by my own clumsy clutching, pulls at resurfacing and incited thought and emotion. The internal witness dredging up the uncompleted missions, the gaping wounds, the unhealed scars, stains the flustered mind and challenges the pristine rite.

Becoming aware of my own moaning, I am sucked downward with a crushing velocity as shredded shards of consciousness plunge back into earth.

I lay eclipsed within the incredulous denseness that is my own body. It is rigid and immovable. Everything is hard and heavy. It feels like it has forgotten to breathe. Struggling for air like a diver emerging from a deep lake, I break the surface as I fight for life-giving breath. The heart is slow, heavy, and uncertain. It intermittently thumps. A cool wind brings the piercing sound of an unknown bird screeching in the distance; or is it the air whistling through the nose and into the lungs.

Everything seems far away and muted. The tongue is thick. The mouth is dry. Eyes don't seem to focus. I decide to sit up. The body doesn't move. It just lays there. Then, suddenly, it jerks back to life. It is tight and awkward. It takes a moment to respond to direction. It is clumsy and stiff. Climbing upward to a sitting position, I continue to breathe the breath of life, instinctively engaging in some yogic pranayama. Eyes begin to water profusely. The nose drips and runs. It appears that I am back. Massaging and stretching my body, a new reverence emerges for the beauty and grace of the temple that our Creator has provided. As strength and coordination slowly return, I follow the setting sun down the sacred mountain.

Arriving home in the valley, I am ready for rest and nourishment. It is good to be back in the arms of my beloved. I stand upon the deck, slowly eating the flesh of fresh cut melon. Its taste is more alive and vibrant than any I've tasted before. Watching the promontory, I remain mesmerized and motionless. It seems I am suspended in time, waiting for something to happen.

After a while the Source debriefs. It explains that the body and consciousness have been heavily taxed, pushed to its limits. It explains that for a while, perhaps months or years, there will be aftershocks, feelings and sensations as there is a readjustment from the events of the day. The Source explains that for a brief moment the centers have flickered and have been opened. It explains that there will be a required time of gentleness with self as the implications and realizations of the experience begin to take hold and blossom within the conscious mind. The conscious view of reality has been profoundly shaken and will never be quite the same again.

After a deep quiet sleep, I awaken, slip on some clothes, and go outside. I am drenched in the light of the glowing moon that permeates everything. It just hangs there, suspended and radiant, neither asking or taking, just being. Its steady undeniable presence illumines my steps. Meandering through the streets, yielding to its delicate flowing, I wander a short distance up onto the hillside, above the lights in the valley. Exploring the illumined darkness, I navigate the rocks, briars and clumps of bunch grass and sit near the outcropping where I had once sought the favor of divine ravens. Recalling the childhood vigil, I remain peacefully astounded by the ever flowing answer.

The long silver-white strands of aspen bark reflect the compassionate moonlight as they rock back and forth with the sighing of caressing breezes. I hear a slow lethargic cadence of some nocturnal explorer. Peering into the direction of the intermittent rustling, I discover the nebulous form of a porcupine waddling across the trail and into the darkness. Brother Owl acknowledges my presence as he leaps from an unseen branch and into silver-feathered flight. Its short wide wings swat at the air as it propels itself into a shadow and disappears. Rocks begin to glow and glisten with the wetness of newly forming dew. Leaves rattle their eternal prayers as my breath rises and falls in unison with pulsing earth.

The heart beats, slowly. Blood pulses laboriously through heavy dense flesh. Muscles are still stiff and seem to respond slowly to the muted suggestions of the will. Aftershocks of the sacred rapture episodically waft through some unseen doorway. Emerging from out of the oneness, the mind is tranquil and still; the heart is content and at peace; the body is nourished and immersed in healing; the soul bears witness to the ever-flowing presence.

There is something there. It is real, alive and mighty. It is totally intimate. It is beyond all conjecture and mythologizing. It is beyond all wondering. It has always been there, even though we are not always able to recognize it. It is nestled within all our blinding layers of trauma. It is a part of and mixed within all our ignorant and arrogant ways of believing and being. It is always there. It is here, now.

Our conscious minds may struggle to devise ideology in order to grasp, comprehend, and manipulate. However, it is not bound by any cult of personality or dogma. It is beyond all petty religiosity and institutionalization. It cannot be induced by credentials or certification. No one has the exclusive franchise. No one book can ever hold its power. No one teacher can have all its answers. Yet its grace and blessings continuously form a progression of sacred vessels that become the foundation of every teacher, doctrine, and religion. It needs no name, but it has been called by many names. It manifests as it will, when it will. Its recognition is the purpose of our existence. It is the essence of our existence. The promises are true.

As the weeks and months pass by, the frequency and intensity begin to subside. However, there are times when the presence is strong. There appears to be a contradiction. For, although you know it is omnipresent, there does not seem to be the ability to continually walk within the beauty that is always there. Old habits, irritants, and the daily scuffle of an irrational society easily squeeze out the conscious recognition. Sometimes a month will go by without a glimmer. Occasionally it buds and blossoms, often in the most unexpected places. Sometimes it seems to come to comfort, to guide, or just to gently remind me that, once again, I have forgotten.

It is acknowledged in others who have also recognized it. I realize I have always been able to recognize it, or have at least sensed it. Some say that once the presence has clearly dawned, it is there for all time. There are claims that one will have vast powers if you have but touched it for a moment. Others claim that those powers can exist without even believing in it, and there may be no powers at all.

I don't know how master yogis and shaman experience it. I only know how I experienced it. Any demanding debate on the subject ultimately smacks of the playful interplay of the duality insisting to know, "Is it this or is it that?" When indulging in the seductive battle of incessant questioning comes the dissecting and the splitting. At these times I am once again drawn back into a shroud of excited irritation or lethargic dullness.

As I continue the path, it becomes clearer and clearer that our lives are indeed a process, not an event; a journey, not a destination. Yes, there are very significant events and turning points along the way. But missed opportunities will often return in other ways. This revealing upon the mountain was a very significant event. And it was foreshadowed by a hundred or maybe a thousand little events, all heralding a moment when the clouds would part and an answer would come.

The maturing traveler begins to realize that our world grows, flows, drifts, and expands in an evolutionary way. Nothing of value comes into being spontaneously. It is planted, sprouts, is nourished, and matures before bringing forth the fruit. Then it often appears to fade away, only to be found growing and flowering in another place, in another time, and in another way. I don't know how it is supposed to be. I only know how I have experienced it.

My suspicion is that it is a consciously growing seed that is capable of taking many forms, but it is always of the one source. My suspicion is that I shall always remain pregnant with the presence of this sacred knowledge as I continue to discover that I have always been wrapped within it, whether I knew it or not. My observation is that it continues as a gentle comforting, guiding and healing, allowing me to progress at my own pace as I am willing and able to accept.

If not pursued, it will probably not come. Yet when it does come, it is a gift that cannot be earned. It is a gift that is eternally given. It has become as a relationship that is a partnership in a constant state of exploration. My hope is that it will continue to grow within me. Whether or not it ever blossoms to the fullest is of no consequence. For it is already here. I know not if there are other levels or other meanings. This seems irrelevant and distracting to the fullness of this one complete and blissful moment.

Although there is continual movement within this motionless quiet, there is no hurry; there is no rush. It moves within each step and within each thought until the journey is ended. It comes again and again to remind me. It coaxes me away from bitterness and calamity. It soothes and caresses. It shares its life with me personally and intimately. It is forever, forgiving. It sends me teachers and helpers. It comes from a place where the human soul may truthfully say, "I am complete and need no more ... ."

Chapter Sixteen

Winds of Change

Within the sacred valley the winds of change were upon us. The leaves were orange-red and yellow. The setting sun was pulling pink and purple-gray hues out of the treeless alpine granite. The presence was strong. As I watched the lengthening shadows, it was decided that a short visit to Bridal Veil Falls would be in order. The mists rising up from the falls are always invigorating and refreshing. As the Jeep rolled past the stop sign, I turned east on Colorado Avenue. I was turning toward the cauldron of creation.

About halfway to the base of the cliffs, I began to feel as if I were expanding and rising above the moving vehicle. I seemed to be both inside and outside of my body at the same time. I parked the Jeep within a grove of shuddering aspen. Stepping from the vehicle, I passed through the open door and fell upon short brown grass that had deep green roots. After a moment of stillness, I faced the promontory and sat in quiet meditation.

Once more I was held within the spell of the Adnipoche. It drew me upward into a cocoon-like vortex. After a few moments the point of consciousness became focused high above the canyon floor. A gentle wave of compassion washed through my being. It seemed protective and motherly. It was as if a slowly moving wind was passing through me, promoting gentle healing, and removing all that was heavy and impure. Drawing like a great magnet, I became absorbed within the sacred promontory.

Then I was seized by a frightful knowing. It filled me with its subtle but terrible message. I was being released from the call that had summoned me to its steep slopes some eight years before. The connection was being severed. My presence was no longer required. As soon as this had been acknowledged, there was a compelling and urgent command to leave the mountain. My mind and emotions questioned and struggled, wanting to deny that this could be true. The three doors of the great citadel were quickly closing in great harmonic unison. It seemed to be wrapping itself within a great protective shroud.

The mandate was unalterably clear. Somehow this sacred center was expelling me from its presence. While it seemed to be pushing me away, it also seemed to catapult itself far off into the distance. There was a sensation of tremendous speed as the gulf between us widened and deepened. It showered me with impressions of a protective mother drawing a ravenous predator away from her children.

It was releasing me from my troth while creating a diversion that the forces of divisiveness would follow. I was being shut out and ordered away from some kind of impending tragedy whose features are yet to be formed. In its own time and in its own way, it was wrapping the impending forces of destruction around itself and preparing for the next stage of its crucifixion. What had been freely offered through grace would now have to be paid for through turmoil and travail.

For the next few days I found myself looking upon everything as if it might be the last time I would ever see it again. This made every experience and every person seem very precious. I found myself studying the face of the mountain, hoping to be able to memorize every rock, every tree, every crevice and waterfall. Each moment appeared as a rapidly fading treasure. Every walk through the town streets, every friendly nod or familiar wave felt like it might be the last.

The days were rapidly flowing. There was a quiet sullenness, a moaning that comes from deep within the soul. It pulled at the presence and drew my attention away from any sense of bliss. These were not happy times. Somehow I cannot or will not accept what had been given. The impact was still wafting its way through the incredulous resistance that had filled my conscious mind. I had finally recovered my paradise, my Garden of Eden. It had taken over forty years to discover and define my one true home. Now I was being told that it was time for leaving. For the first time in my life I felt as if I were not working toward something, but that I was running away from something. This would be a very difficult path to walk. Once more, I was being cast out of the garden.

During the next few weeks the mind began questioning the intensity and validity of this incredulous experience. Perhaps it was something symbolic. Maybe I was misinterpreting. If leaving Telluride was truly an option, it would surely be much better to wait until both children had graduated from high school. Perhaps it was merely some kind of flashback, the kind of thing the Source had warned me about. The kind of thing that happens when the centers have been opened and then flounder in confusion in attempts to make sense of the experience and to re-establish some kind of balance around some stable points of earthly reference.

If there was any reason to take this experience literally, there would surely come some channeled guidance or direction. However, this had become one of those long periods of time in which the Source remained silent. During occasional peaceful moments, the familiar bliss once again began to weave its comforting way back into the daily consciousness. It seemed that perhaps things were slowly getting back to normal.

It had been a good morning for some long, slow yogic stretching. Settling peacefully into one of my favorite postures, time had become suspended. With prana-filled breath, the air within my lungs felt rich, nourishing, and full of life. Descending from the sadhana loft, I began rattling around in the refrigerator in quest of my daily allotment of fresh orange juice. It seemed the perfect transition from the early morning meditation. Walking through the doors and out upon the deck, I found myself peering into the vanishing darkness of a new day. My eyes began to ravage the morning beauty of the sacred mountain as I sipped the orange nectar from my favorite porcelain cup. Then I began to feel a familiar presence. The air grew heavy and intense and seemed to vibrate.

From behind me came a stern and commanding voice, "Sir!"

I turned my head and there He stood. It was the voice of the Elder Brother, the one that I would know as Lord and Messiah. This was one whose power, compassion, and wisdom is capable of embracing all the ages, races, teachings, and paths. This was the Adnam, first born of the Creator. Before I had a chance to question or ponder, the voice continued.

"It is time for you to leave; complete the mandate, fulfill your mission. Share with others that which you have been given. This is the way; this is your path. When your time has ended, I shall come for you."

Sometimes I wish that it hadn't happened this way. There are few who would believe that such events are even possible, let alone true. Yet this is the way it was. It is the way it is remembered. Some will say that such events are just made up. Others will say these are merely the deluded reflections and hallucinations of an unbalanced mind. Some will be touched, quickened, and inspired. And some will know the story to be true, for they too have spent time in pilgrimage upon the sacred promontories within mountains that shine.

It is not for me to question or decide how the reader shall respond to the story. It is only my responsibility to share the story. It is the story of my questing upon the sacred mountain that called out to me and set my feet upon a sacred journey. It is only one story of many. It is only one way of many. It is but a footprint of one pilgrim upon a highway of pilgrims. But sometimes as we journey, it is good to know that others have come this way. It is good to know that there is life, light, and magic. It is good to know that there are still sacred mountains, holy pilgrimages, angels, gods, and sacred teachings.

*   *   *   *   *

The Source has become a rare visitor who claims that now would come a time for us to learn to stand on our own two feet, follow our own personal connection and intuitive guidance, and move into the next phase of our journey. We continued with the pleasures and obligations of the householder and watched our children grow into their own adulthood. Now I have become a grandfather.

Sometimes I spend a quiet evening out under the stars, sprawled out upon the land, nestling close to Earth Mother. Sometimes I am caught up in the majesty of a slowly moving rain storm, or found marveling at the miracle of a shimmering rainbow. Sometimes I simply rest in the rapture of a cozy shadow. There are occasional visits from fellow pilgrims who wish to maintain contact and contemplate life's mystical adventures. Sometimes there are hints that there shall be other adventures when the time is right. Sometimes I am granted a short pilgrimage to nourish and be nourished at the place of initiation within the holy citadel.

Now another year has ended. And I am finally completing this chronicle of my experience upon the mountain. Life continues with its frustrations, opportunities, and challenges. Not long ago my beloved made her final transition, just as her source had hinted at on so many occasions. Long was the preparation and gentle was her passing. Though she is gone, often do I feel her loving presence, smiling upon me. Someday I may endeavor to tell her wondrous story.

Although there are still precious moments, the visions have dissipated and the visitations have faded. The blissful consciousness remains, but it has become a timid intermittent stream that flows quietly in the background. During the frustration and machinations of the day, it is too often ignored or forgotten. But when called upon or, perhaps more accurately, when it is acknowledged, it always seems to be there, gently nurturing and guiding a weary but awakening soul. It serves as an eternal barometer and witness to the magic and mystery of a Creator that lives within an ever-evolving universe.

We migrated northward near a place that the Source calls Zimba Ba'avaché. It is a place of ducks, geese, and hawks. It is a place where deer reach into the edges of urban civilization. They often spend their nights nestled in deep grass that is surrounded by wild olive trees. It is a place where packs of coyotes can be heard howling through the darkness. It is a place where an occasional bear is spotted and sometimes a footprint of the cougar is found within moist sand.

We settled beneath tall green trees near ruddy red cliffs of the swirling mesa that lies northwest of the city. The great circle of our fourth migration has been completed. Now I prepare for the onslaught of winter where I shall wait for the birth of the fifth world and the beginning of a new migration.

Now there has begun another kind of pilgrimage, a quest to wrestle a few glowing embers from the ashes of Celtic and Nordic ancestors. If the breath of life can reignite our pagan fires, then perhaps the flames will be bright enough to weave new fibers into an ancient tapestry. Perhaps I shall once again merge with the great mysteries and cycles of life and reclaim a place within the sacred circle. Now is the time to gather ancient seed and preserve it for future planting and harvesting. This is seed that will come forth after the melting of the purifying snows that will accompany the impending winter.

As I complete these pages, the rocks from the sweat lodge are still warm. There is an attempt to pattern it after the traditions of those who practiced the batsu and savusana in a place that was once called Scandia. A small blue cross with a circle around it dangles within the center of the lodge. Although it has been anointed as the symbol of a risen christ, it shall always remind me of the sun wheel of Wodan, our Allfather. The smell of sage still clings to my hair and body. Prayer feathers of crimson, gold, and violet adorn the sacred grove in the midst of sacred space. It is good to live in this special place. I have been greatly blessed by the wisdom of its changing seasons, through its tragedy as well as its inspiration.

I once again find myself contemplating the many events of the last few years during my tutelage upon the mountain. It is good to begin the process of rediscovering ancient heritage.

It is good to remember that our white ancestors were great pagan warriors, shaman, and explorers who reveled in the cruel fierceness, raging passion, and gentle healing of Earth Mother in all of her wondrous moods.

It is good to walk within the presence of gods and angels. It is good to remember that our people are an essential part of the great circle of pagan nations. It is good to be a born again pagan and to know that the messianic force is real and comes with many friends and helpers. It is good to know that it comes to heal and strengthen the many clans.

It is good to know that He was sent from a heavenly Father that honors the always present and nurturing goddess of sanctified Earth. It is good to know that the Father comforts the Mother, and that the Mother empowers the Father. It is good to know that She shall always rise from the ashes with the redeeming power of crucified Earth and bask in the brilliance of the rising Sun. It is good to know that there are stories that are yet to be lived. It is good to know that there is a place for me when my time is finished. It is good to know that my beloved has found her place among the stars.

Now the story is written and you have shared in some of the knowledge that I have gained upon this path. As this chronicle of my time upon the mountain is completed, I wish you wondrous peace and glorious adventures. Perhaps one day we shall pass one another while on pilgrimage, walking along an ancient trail, chanting a prayer of joy and appreciation. Perhaps we shall meet within the highlands of a magnificently shining mountain, or deep within an enchanted grove, or wading through healing waters that flow through the sacred valley.

Epilogue

Late
last night
deep within
that realm of realms

More tangible
more vivid
more alive
than ordinary reality

A valkyrian goddess
came to me
embracing me eagerly
bringing warm lips close
to anxious hungry ears
whispering gently
her bold rapturous message

"I wish you no harm
but, I can resist no longer

I am mesmerized
I am overflowing
within the wake
of the boundless passion
of your relentless questing

I have always been
here …

Beside the river
waiting patiently
for you to remember

Waiting faithfully
since the beginning
for your resurrection

Longing eternally
in anticipation
of your radiant return

Deep within your heart
I want you to know
if you have need of me
I am here …

I will be your concubine
I will be your mistress
I will be your lover

And when our time is over
I shall always be
here—with you …

Drifting within
unleashed writhing wind

Glowing within
hot raging fire

Flowing within
trembling luminous waters

Growing within
sacred moaning earth

And
I shall rejoice
forever … "

This was a dream I had
by the waterfall
within the valley
of the Rajh Adnipoche …

Glossary of Uncommon Terminology

Adesh   The spiritual name provided to the author, which supposedly describes the essence of his soul's nature and purpose. It has to do with bridging the rift between different planes of consciousness. It also relates to that which exudes forth from the primal forces of creation.

Adnam   First born of the Creator. The one who broke the circle and led his people into the earth and subsequently has the honor and responsibility to lead his people back to the circle once more. The polestar of creation. The anointed one, the risen Christ.

Adnipoche   The term used by the Source to identify any of the five primal earth chakras. Although it sounds Tibetan or Buddhist, the root meaning supposedly predates these more modern languages. Rahj Adnipoche is the name given by the author to the primal center within the Telluride region.

Allfather   The name of the reigning god of the Nordic pantheon, often meaning all-father or val-father, from Valhalla, the Nordic version of a heavenly afterworld.

Allah   The Muslim name for God.

Antichrist   That which actively opposes the natural will of God. Believed by some to be an actual entity—angel, kachina, demon or spirit—that will eventually incarnate and wreak havoc and destruction in the world. *See also* Pagan.

Armageddon   A shallow valley located in the Middle East where Christian doctrine proclaims there will be a final earthly battle between the forces of good and evil. *See also* Ragnarok.

Asanas   A name for the physical postures or positions that are assumed during the practice of yoga.

Ashram   A name for a place where a community of people seeks spiritual growth through personal instruction and aspires to live a lifestyle based upon a set of specific principles and practices.

Astral   Refers to the next plane of material existence where ghosts and spirits supposedly dwell. It is believed that the soul inhabits a spirit body, which in turn inhabits the physical or flesh body. The bodies interact through the chakras. Some teachings claim that there may be as many as ten sheaths that wrap the soul and occupy the various planes of existence. Upon death, it is possible that a soul may become attached to any one of these levels or move between one or more levels. Moving beyond these levels and "into the light" is ultimately the proper place for a discarnate soul.

Auric   From aura, which is the subtle life force that some people can actually see. Many consider this to be the halo, which is often depicted in paintings of angels or saints. It may consist of a wide variety of color combinations and displays that surround the physical body. Some claim to be able to tell much about a person from viewing the aura.

A photographic process called Kirlean photography has been developed in which this energy can be seen emanating from living things. However, whether or not it is the actual aura is controversial. Some claim the true aura is only in the mind of the psychic.

Batsu   Another term for a type of sweat lodge that was once used by a reindeer-herding people of the northern Arctic.

Brigadoon   The name of a legendary magical kingdom that manifests on our earthly plane for a short period of time every few hundred years.

Buddha   A spiritual leader who lived in India. His teachings became the foundation of the Buddhist religion. An illumined one is sometimes referred to as a Buddha.

Cessna   Manufacturer of a line of small aircraft built primarily for private use.

Chakra   One of several centers of energy located within planetary as well as physical bodies that are believed to be associated with certain mystical powers. Their overall harmony and balance maintains general health and well-being. The centers can be used as gateways to other planes and dimensions of consciousness, which may ultimately result in spiritual enlightenment or illumination. *See also* Kundalini.

Dakini   For the purpose of this book, a reference to the Tibetan Buddhist pantheon of spirits and supernatural beings that represent the elemental forces of nature. Also known as sprites, elves, trolls, and fairies. Some are reputed to have substantial magical powers that are used to keep the natural world in a state of order and harmony.

Dharma   The particular path or set of teachings that one embraces in order to seek spiritual fulfillment. Also used to refer to a particular person's prescribed lifestyle or set of circumstances from which one can learn and gain insight and thereby grow into spiritual maturity.

Dutch oven   A heavy cast-iron pot with a loose fitting lid that can be used in an open fire for the purpose of baking.

El Dorado   A legendary city of vast treasures sought by the Spanish explorers and conquistadors. Indian legends fueled this European obsession. It was believed to be located in South America or in the American Southwest. Also referred to as the Seven Cities of Gold.

Elementals   The four primary forces of nature: air, fire, water, and earth. The multitudes of spirit beings that hover about and interact with the physical world. *See also* Dakini.

Elks Club   A social and community service organization that was extremely popular in the small communities of the Rocky Mountains.

Enemy Way   The cultural or philosophical perspective that requires an opponent or enemy in order to justify its existence, thereby providing itself with purpose and meaning.

Enlightenment   A profound state of awareness and insight into things of a spiritual nature. *See also* illumination.

Ethereal   Sometimes referred to as the causal level of existence. Usually considered to be within or beyond the higher astral levels. *See also* Aura.

Freyja   An ancient Nordic goddess often associated with magic, the cycles of nature, and eroticism. Sometimes a defender of the hearth and home. Also known as a protector and guardian of travelers and the portals through which various forms of existence can be explored.

Guru   That which brings light into darkness. In recent times, it has come to mean a teacher of considerable knowledge and ability. Also, one's personal teacher and recognized embodiment of divine authority. One's personal teacher is often called sadh or "true" guru. Guru dev refers to a center or rallying point of divine grace, usually one's teacher.

Guruji   A term expressing familiarity and affection for one's Guru.

Hopi   The name of a Native American, pueblo-dwelling people in northern Arizona. Originally spelled Moki, the name is often represented as meaning the "the peaceful people."

Illumination   That ultimate state of being, which is in complete communion with and totally filled by that divine presence that we sometimes call God. *See also* Enlightenment.

Inipi   The North American Plains Indian name for a sweat lodge. *See also* Batsu and Sava-sauna.

Jeshua ben Joseph   The Hebrew name of the one who is now known as Jesus. He is reputed to have become the Christ personified and is the central figure of most Christian religions.

Jnana or Gyana   A name for the dharma or spiritual path that seeks spiritual fulfillment by exploring the nature of mind and levels of consciousness. Through the quest for truth, with sincerity and commitment, one discovers firsthand knowledge, which can lead to wisdom and enlightenment.

Kachina   The name of the physical personifications of the traditional spirit beings of the Southwestern pueblo peoples. They are similar to angels and elementals in their purpose and function. They are closely linked to specific rituals and ceremonies in which their powers are recognized, called upon, and honored.

Kiva   The pueblo Indian name for any structure where sacred ceremonies are conducted. Kivas are most often underground and circular. Sometimes natural earth features are inhabited for these purposes. Topographical shapes are often seen as emblematic of the predominant forces and spiritual energies present in a certain region or location. The most common use of the term describes a man-made structure. The particular clan or group of individuals that conducts specific ceremonies or rituals for the benefit of their people may be referred to as a kiva or a society.

Kriya   The name for certain yogic practices, which cleanse the body and promote good health. In a more esoteric sense, it is any specified grouping of practices, often arcane or secret, that promote physical, emotional, and mental cleansing in preparation for a higher state of consciousness and general well-being.

Kundalini   The name of the power or force, usually seen as a tangible spiritual energy, that rises through the chakras of the physical body from the base of the spine through the top of the head. Some believe that this force is always there, and the rising is just the conscious recognition of its presence. This often occurs during a profound episode of spiritual awakening. Some mythologists believe it is only symbolic. The description of the Pentecost in the Bible has been likened to the rising of the kundalini force with the descriptions of tongues of fire above the heads of the illumined.

Many believe that it can only be successfully awakened through the precise mastery of specific yogic practices. Others believe that this is a common experience that most souls encounter no matter what their particular path, practices, or dogma. The proper application of certain combinations of natural drugs used in shamanic rituals is said to be able to accomplish the same thing. There is sometimes concern that forcing the chakras to open through the use of drugs, or the practice of kundalini yoga, when the person has not attained the appropriate spiritual balance and development, can result in death, dementia, or insanity. For this reason, it is sometimes seen as a dangerous and even satanic force associated with witchcraft or evil.

There are stories of those who claim they have recognized that they have pushed the release of kundalini energy beyond the capacity of the physical body to handle it, and subsequently no longer have the capacity to make the "blissful connection" because they have damaged their auric and ethereal bodies beyond repair. They supposedly wait for yet another incarnation and a new physical body to continue their practices. Still others consider such stories preposterous and feel that such ideas are the result of grotesque superstition and ignorance.

Lana-lahti   A personal song, story, or other creative work, which is a reflection or witness to one's spiritual journey.

Mantra   A repetitive sound or chant that is used to focus or relax the mind, body, and emotions in order to become more centered and in tune with spiritual forces. The presentation of a mantra is often used as a device for initiation and may be the beginning of personal instruction with a teacher. The actual syllables or sounds can be selected as a precise prescription for a particular need or may reflect a simple prayer or blessing of good will. Many believe the most powerful mantra is the beating of a pure and innocent heart belonging to a devoted seeker of truth.

Nordic skis   The traditional long, wide snow skis that were developed in the Scandinavian countries. They were usually attached to one's footgear by a harness or strapping made of leather.

Pagan   Refers to the ancient worldview that creation is not only a manifestation of god, but that god and the wisdom of god are embodied within the physical world. Subsequently, there is a natural system of birth, growth, harvest, and death cycles that eternally demonstrate and promote that harmony and balance within a limitless universe full of beauty and challenge.

That which we would call god manifests in many different ways, in many different places, depending on the needs and creativity of the times. However, there is ultimately one source and one creator of the many peoples, many cultures, and many gods. The basic principles always remain the same. Everything, including humankind, is an essential part of this all-encompassing drama.

That which is truly evil seeks to deny and unseat the balance and destroy the harmony through the belief that god exists somewhere outside of creation and that, by accident or on purpose, god created parts of the universe that are inherently corrupt and need to be conquered and permanently restrained or destroyed.

Prana   Means breath; but more than this, it is the magical substance within the air that animates all things and makes them alive, radiant, and powerful.

Prashad   An edible treat or gift symbolizing being fed and nourished through the grace of the Creator. It is often offered to devotees or parishioners in ceremony or ritual. Some consider it to be similar to the more complex Christian ceremony of eucharistic communion.

Pranayama Yogic practices in which the breath is manipulated, controlled, and directed in order to improve health and bring a sense of well-being to body, mind, emotions, and spirit.

Ragnarok The Nordic name for the final mythic battle referred to by Christians as Armageddon. *See also* Armageddon.

Rastafarian A follower of the late Haile Selassie, King of Ethiopia, who some believe was a messiah. Converts are usually identified by wearing a hairstyle of long, matted curls, usually referred to as "dreadlocks." The use of cannabis sativa is considered to be a sacrament. However, some claim that this use of sacramental marijuana has become excessive and is generally abused. Most see this as a religion of the black race, however, other races are often welcome to participate. Although concrete doctrine is hard to find, there seems to be a general belief that the promised land is on the African continent.

Sadhana One's spiritual practices, which usually occur on a daily basis and may include such things as the reading of scripture, prayer, meditation, yoga, chanting, etc.

Sally port An area within a corrections facility that contains more than one door and consequently controls inmate movement by providing that only one of two required doors is opened at a time, thereby restricting the possibility of escape by bolting through a single door.

Sanghat A group of people that share common ideas and practices in their quest for truth and spiritual enlightenment. A congregation of truthseekers.

Sava-sauna Another name for a sweat lodge used by the Nordic people from Scandia.

Scandia The ancient name of that area of northwestern Europe, which is now called Scandinavia, and includes the countries of Norway, Sweden, Denmark, and sometimes Iceland. The former lands of the Nordic peoples that reached throughout northern Europe.

Sevakhra A bracelet worn for the purpose of identification and commemoration of a commitment to a certain spiritual path or dharma.

Shaman A practitioner of pagan religion that has the capacity, through ceremony, visions, and insight to bridge the gap between the seen and unseen worlds in order to establish and augment balance and harmony for the people they serve. They are most often seen as working with the supernatural as both priest/priestess and physician, such as a Native American Indian medicine man/woman, and may be expert herbalists.

Shangri-la A magical kingdom or paradise on earth whose location is unknown or hidden from the rest of the world.

Shiva A god of the Hindu pantheon. Emblematic of the process of harvesting or returning to the Creator. Sometimes seen as the "patron saint" or ultimate practitioner or source of the practice of Yoga, which reconnects the seeker to divine presence.

Sikh A monotheistic tradition founded in India by Guru Hanak several hundred years ago.

Sita-Ram Ram is an energy pattern personifying truth, righteousness, and virtue. Sita is the feminine aspect, which balances Ram. Chanted together as a mantra, they can be said to embody or inspire an ideal marriage or union of the dual and cooperative aspects of one's persona.

Snow-blind   The common name for a condition in which the ability of the retina of the eye to differentiate between different shades of light becomes "bleached out" due to prolonged exposure to continuous bright light, such as manifested in a snow field. The condition can be painful, but it usually clears up within a few days without permanent damage.

Source   The name given for the source of information that was channeled through the author's wife. It supposedly comes from that realm where the individual soul merges with the universal consciousness of all creation. It allegedly manifests from that point, drawing upon a vast network of information and experience. Occasionally, it may include entities, spirits, and angels who may have an interest in or special relationship with those who are being addressed through the Source. At times the information can be distorted by the attitudes and emotions of the channel and/or those who are seeking information. If conditions are not optimal, the Source tends to temporarily withdraw. The Source has supposedly been known by many names throughout the ages. It has manifested in a multitude of earthly expressions, depending upon the needs and circumstances of those being served. Every person apparently has the potential to make contact with this universal consciousness.

Stockholm Syndrome   The name given to a psychological phenomena in which people, who are held hostage or in close proximity to people whose views are radically different from their own, tend to develop a pattern of adopting and supporting what was previously a completely alien and hostile point of view.

Swami   A term for a Hindu monk and/or spiritual teacher.

Swamiji   A term describing familiarity and affection for a specific Hindu monk. Can be considered as an individual recognition of one who is providing valuable personal teachings.

Sweat lodge   The common American term for a sacred ceremony in which one utilizes certain arcane knowledge and rituals in the process of cleansing one's body, mind, and emotions. One generally retreats to a secluded location where a small dome-shaped structure has been constructed. When ready, carefully tended rocks that have been heated in an open fire are placed within the darkened lodge. During the ceremony, water is poured over the hot and usually glowing stones. This creates an intimate steam bath where participants congregate for purification, healing, and instruction.

Talking circles   A generic term for practices in which people come together in a circle and participate in conversation that usually has a particular purpose or theme that may not always be obvious at the beginning. A sacred object of some kind, such as a feather, decorated stick, gourd, or rock crystal, is passed around. The only one allowed to talk is the one who holds the object. Such sessions can promote unity, consensus, and insight regarding the particular problems or needs of the group.

Tantra   A spiritual philosophy often accompanied by specialized technical information and practices that form a path for rapid attainment of spiritual enlightenment or illumination. The foundation is often believed to have originated with Tibetan Buddhists. Some feel the concepts and technology are much older.

Originally, there were three major branches. White tantric yoga tended to deal with righteous living and purpose, which some would term puritanical. There was an emphasis on recognizing and balancing the male and female aspects within ourselves and our communities and within nature in general. Many postures and exercises were used, as well as intellectual knowledge and practical applications of meditative skills.

Black tantric yoga generally dealt with magical powers and spells, demonology, and witchcraft, that attempted to gain control and domination over others. It eventually fell into disrepute and was considered to be evil.

Red tantric yoga is what most recognize today and has to do with explicate sexual practices and exercises, which are believed to enhance consciousness and the process toward enlightenment. However, the technology is most often used for the purposes of enhancing physical pleasure.

Telluride A small town in southwestern Colorado that became a major ski resort where this autobiographical story unfolds.

Third eye The name of the chakra, centered in and around the pituitary gland within the forehead, which is a symbolic and literal connection to other planes of consciousness. It represents the pathway to spiritual power and knowledge. It is sometimes referred to as the master gland for physiological as well as esoteric reasons.

Thor One of the gods of the Nordic pantheon who epitomized strength, power, and courage in the defense of tribe and clansmen. He is sometimes referred to as the god of thunder and lighting and swings a mighty hammer in defense of the righteous.

Tickling the Dragon's Tail A phrase making reference to tempting fate, pushing oneself past one's abilities and placing oneself in unnecessary danger. The dragon hereby being emblematic of great power, but also tending to much arrogance and misdirected ego.

Troth An absolutely solemn pledge that is freely given and may not be broken without the most dire of consequences.

Valkyrie The legendary Nordic goddesses who would come into the world as devouring, scavenging ravens and return fallen warriors to the heavenly world called Valhalla.

Wodan The Allfather of the Nordic pantheon. Also spelled as Odin. *See also* Allfather.

Yahweh The name given to the ancient Hebrew god, also known as Jehovah.

Yarrow A hardy, bluish-green plant with compound leaves and pure white flowers. Sometimes used by Nordic shaman to enhance clarity of vision, insight, and purpose.

Yoga Means union and refers in a generic sense to any activity that promotes the merging of the individual with the supreme soul, which is god. Generally refers to physical postures and exercises used to strengthen the body, calm the emotions, and focus the mind in the quest for spiritual fulfillment.

Zimba Ba'avaché The name given by the Source to that area northwest of Grand Junction, Colorado, most commonly known as the Colorado National Monument.

Zuni The name of a pueblo-dwelling people of northern New Mexico.

When a society or civilization perishes,
one condition can always be found.
They forgot where they came from.

Carl Sandburg